ZODIAC

KENT

Edited by Lucy Jeacock

First published in Great Britain in 2002 by
YOUNG WRITERS
Remus House,
Coltsfoot Drive,
Peterborough, PE2 9JX
Telephone (01733) 890066

HB ISBN 0 75433 638 7
SB ISBN 0 75433 639 5

FOREWORD

Young Writers was established in 1991 with the aim of promoting creative writing in children, to make reading and writing poetry fun.

Once again, this year proved to be a tremendous success with over 41,000 entries received nationwide.

The Zodiac competition has shown us the high standard of work and effort that children are capable of today. The competition has given us a vivid insight into the thoughts and experiences of today's younger generation. It is a reflection of the enthusiasm and creativity that teachers have injected into their pupils, and it shines clearly within this anthology.

The task of selecting poems was a difficult one, but nevertheless, an enjoyable experience. We hope you are as pleased with the final selection in *Zodiac Kent* as we are.

CONTENTS

Carly Maunsell   1

Bexley Grammar School
Michael Palmer	2
William Attard	2
Kelsey Williams	3
Joshua Clipsham	4
Charlotte Newton	4
Monica Kalinska-Bialek	5
Nathan Aspell	5
Damilola Bajomo	6
Calvin Woodroffe	6
Monica Patel	7
Cleo Harris	8
Lois Wallace	9
Lewis Anderson	9
Inderveer Singh Salh	10
Jean-Paul Mascarenhas	11
Ian Witsey	12
Sarah Wildblood	12
Jake Gowers	13
Matthew Jenkins	13
Charnpreet Minhas	14
Lauren Bartlett	15
Ben Church	16
Daniel Jones	16
Anthony Macina	17
Daniel Wendon	17
Joseph Tinlin	18
Chantelle Simper	18
Jennifer Hien	19
George Unitt	19
Philip Bayley	20
Daniel Burns	21
Lara Williams	22
Harriet Coombs	22

Faye Highland   23
Amanda Ly   23
Alexandra Tolfree   24
Samantha Cefai   24
Tolu Elebiju   25
Emily Downs   25
Gurdeep Briah   26
Ella Gardiner   26
Connor Gorrard-Smith   27
Sonita Baker   27
Stacey Phipps   28
Sam Fisher   28
Charlie Tennent   29
Joe Simpson   29
Jeff Riza   30
Daniel Sydee   30
Hanaa Neetoo   31
Daniel Burn Webster   31
Philip Gosling   31
Thomas Hart   32
Peter Willson   32
Sophie Haslam   33
Samuel Ly   33
Amit Bhanderi   33

Charles Darwin School
Clare Allen   34
Stephanie O'Brien   35
Rachel Schafer   36
Daniel Slade   37
Stephen Peneycad   38

Christ Church CE High School
Claire Archer   38
Lee Fishlock   39
Mathew Tippett   40
Hannah Verlinden   40
Karen Thatcher   41

Kayleigh Offen   42
Howard Cockram   42
Barry Fannon   43
Marie Brough   43
Lucy Kingsnorth   44
Paul Barford   45
Clive Chittenden   46

Dover Grammar School For Girls
Hannah Dring   46
Catherine Johnston   47
Elizabeth Pooley   48
Caroline Rose   48
Emily Hazrati   49
Ruth Marlow   49
Sophie Gray   50
Natasha Clinch   50
Niccy Mounteney   51
Amy Collier   51
Chloe Carr   52
Wahida Islam   52
Lindsay Kennett   53
Anieka Saxby   53
Charlotte Vines   54
Emily O'Hare   54
Fauve Fendt   55
Michelle Downey   56
Nicola Pollard   56
Ria Sandilands   57
Carla Petch   58
Samantha Taylor   58
Megan Jones   59
Katie Phillips   60
Sian Spicer   60
Carys Nia Williams   61
Michelle Simmons   62
Yazmin Fisher   62
Rachel Attryde   63

Emma Cowens	63
Alex Topping	64
Amy Connolly	64
Jennifer Byrne	65
Toniann Magrino-Daly	65
Samantha Horrobin	66
Kellie Weaver	66
Dawn Glover	67
Jodie Beer	68
Laurence Biot	68
Amy Cole	69
Kelly James	70
Alys Hewer	70
Nicola Reed	71
Rachel McGarry	72
Katie Clarke	73
Antara Banerjee	74
Suzanne Jones	74
Heather Goodsell	75
Victoria Keeler	75
Alex Phillips	76
Chelsea Ramsay	76
Hannah Langley	77
Megan Landman	77
Roxanne Skone	78
Natalie Dowle	79
Hollie Humphries	80
Samantha Holness	80
Francesca Parsons	81
Stacey Salter	82
Kelly Jarvis	82
Danielle Henry	83
Sonia Woolls	84
Rebecca McMahon	84
Kylie Scott	85
Amy Smallridge-Smith	86
Dorinda Calvo	86
Kiri Gordon	87

Katie Price	87
Imogen Vasey	88
Kimberley Smith	89
Jessica Little	90
Laura Patton	91
Louise Revell	92
Hannah Dixon	92
Rachael Fletcher	93
Lisa Howard	94
Abigail Tyler	95
Hannah Kelly	96
Danielle Hammond	96
Shannon King	97
Victoria Bates	97
Louise Campbell	98
Sarah Trafford	98
Ellie Cox	99
Rosie Cracknell	100
Megan Georgiou	100
Lucy Perrow	101
Natalie Georgiou	102
Sophie Wolfenden	102
Anna-Nadia Tweed	103
Jade Everett	104
Catherine Renault	105
Kathryn Williams	106
Rebecca Grew	106
Emma Hodge	107
Helen Nolan	107
Hollie Lee	108
Hannah Taylor	109
Maria Duran	110
Kimberley Turner	110
Elizabeth Morton Baged	111
Helen Stubbs	111
Gina Winthrop	112
Leah Baker	113

Hartsdown Technology College

Alan Dewsnap	113
Alisha Dixon	114
James Heathorn	114
Marc Wood	115
Andrew Parker	115
Benjy Smith	115
Daniel Akhurst	116
Andrew Bennette	116
Kimberley Elmes	116
Luke Adams	117
Kerry Mann-Taylor	117
Ysabelle Bradshaw	118
Sean Robinson	118
Tim McArthur	119
Christopher Marsh	119
Carrie Couldridge	120
Sarah Burnett	120
Kirsty Ramshead	121
Shane O'Connor	122
Douglas Sinclair	122
Natasha Collins	123
Abby Scarr	124
Caroline Crouch	124
Vicky Mann	125
Matthew Shurmer	126
Clare Vincer	126
Hayley Kelly	127
Rebecca Spencer	127
Lawrence Hollett	128
Clare Stevens	128
Simon White	129
Victoria Britton	130
Ian Swift	130
Hannah Skull	131
Jodie Bing	131
Scott Young	132
Lauren Edwards	132

Charity Styles	133
Samantha Howard	133
Carly Winter	134
Ben Newman	134
Kieran Cox	135
Rochelle Mandeville	135
Portia Godden	136
Christopher Lane	137
Janine Judd	138
Donna Lehan	138
Martin Ventham	138
Chanelle Stevens	139
Jessica Blake	139
James Walker	140
David Margrave	140
Kirsty Beddows	140
Stacey Tompsett	141
Mary Gonella	141
Charlotte Perry	142
Aimee Penfold	142
Matthew Parker	143
Lawrence Wolf	143
Matthew Coles	143
Aaron Arniszewski	144
Florence Gentle-Spens	145
Kerry Vella	146
Hayley Taylor	146
Ben Akhurst	147
Michael Atkins	147
Richard Lane	148
Scott Francis	148
Ricky Davies	148
Richard Pownall	149
Saima Yousuf	149
Abigail Faulkner	149
Ben Catt	150
Nicole Grant	150
Ruth Stone	151

Ella Chapman	152
Katrina Marney	152
Carina Banham	153
Emily Newman	154
Michael Fay	154
Michael Lambert	155
Kate Hearsey	156
Sarah Greves	156
Stacey Nicholls	156
Michaela Hawkins	157
Jade Thrumble	157
Lauren Miles	158
Stephen Stroud	158
Michelle Male	159
Sophie Healy	160
Mark Page	160
Laura Mitchell	161
Aaron Rushton	161
Abby Saunders	162
Andrew Lockyer	162
Andrew Blackburn	162
Natalie Moore	163
Lauren Lipscomb	163
Nicholas Haynes	164
Ryan Riddell-Broomfield	164
Philip Quigley	165
Sheryl Martin	165
Samantha Overy	166

Highworth Grammar School

Fiona Scoble	166
Clare Hammond	167
Samantha Smith	167
Claire Linkins	168
Charlotte Linter	169
Laura Pizzey	170
Rachael Abbott	171

Sarah Worsley   172
Charliene Keen   173
Anna Fodor   174
Claire Cartwright   175
Emma Murray   176
Zana Beasley   176
Hermione Jones   177
Bethany Dearlove   178

Langley Park School For Boys
James Parascandolo   178
Paul Taylor   179
David Plummer   180
Adam Jones   181
Duncan Shadbolt   182
Russell Warner   183
Mark Hayzer   184
Liam Norval   185
Jeremy Farr   186
Ian Mooney   186
William Bishop   187
Andrew Botten   187
Joseph Aswani   188
Matthew Hutchinson   188
Sean Fabri   189
Edward Newman   189
Jack Stevens   190
Aaron Sparkes   190
Michael Blair   191
Anthony Pike   191
Asanka Weeratunge   192
Richard Legate   192
Daniel O'Connor   193
Luke Richards   193
Nick Pelling   194
Jonathan Michael Roberts   194
Nicholas Wakeling   195

Jamie Gibbons	196
Thomas McLaren	196
Andrew Straiton	197
Ricky Cella	198
Ben McLaren	199
Luke Robertson	200
Pierre Connell	201
Jonathan Davis	202
Alex Leone	203
James Bran	204
James Nattrass	205
Faraz Auckbarally	206
Tejus Patel	208
Luke Bassett	209
Richard Lewis	210
Tom Shingles	211
Josh Mills	212
Ravi Patel	213
Oliver Holden-Rea	214
Alex Balbastro	215
Michael O'Hanlon	216
Christopher Glover	216
Joseph McCloskey	217
Paul Howes	218
David Straiton	219
David Carter	220
Alexander McNeill	221
Thomas McClinton	222
Adam Peters	223
Edward Feist	224
Tim Kay	225
Anthony Plummer	226
Matthew Vadis	227
David Hayes	228
Cyprian Rangel	229
David Jani	230
Robert Outram	231

Stephen Banfield   232
Jack Martin   233
Keir Ferguson   234
Nicholas Brabner   235
Daniel Leeves   236
Matthew Clayton   237
Rowan Lonsdale   238
Alex Batten   238
Sam Hudson   239
Sam Sunderland   239
Daniel Watson   240
Daniel Malynn   240
Christopher Lesflores   241
Joseph Sutcliffe   241
James Wilson   242
James King   243
Matthew Howard   244
Michael Quigley   245
Timothy Burton   246
Steven Eadon   248
Robbie Mathieson   250

Marjorie McClure School
Vimal Patel   250
Caraline Thompson   251
Francesca Duff   252

St Anselm's Catholic School, Canterbury
Hannah Louise Payne   252
Sophia Moffatt-White   253
Bethany Clegg   254
Dominic Alexander   254
Charlotte Stiffell   255
Jack Martyn   255
Giselle Hyam   256
Natalie Shilling   257
Victoria King   258

Josephine Kirwan	259
Sophie Wood	260
Liam Bestic	260
Ashley Dadd	261
Helen Underwood	261
Asti Speed	262
Jessica Driscoll	262
Emma Benson	263
Rosie Burgess	263
Jonathan Murray	264
Sophie Cartwright	264
Ryan Smith	265
Jonathan Hoyle	265
Joe Vallely	266
Mark Fellowes	266
Robert Coles	267
Rosanna Hosker-Thornhill	267
Lauren Morgan	268
Michael Baker	268
Hannah Wilford	269

The Cedars Pru School

Simone Brazier	269
Tomos Lewis	270
Daniel Macken	270
Phillip Fagg	271

King Ethelbert School

Rebecca Halls	271
Gregory Bayliss	272
Kayleigh Maxted	272
Amy Stevens	273
James Tomlinson	274
Jessica Dempsey	274
Samantha Taylor	275
Jodie Gee	276
Kelly Marshall	276

Jessica Pettman 277
Lucy Cook 278
Hayley Constable 278
William Mitchell 279
Kelly Marshall 280
Natalie Jones 280

Westwood Technology College
Julie-Anne Whitaker 281
Louis Smith 281
Julie Cairncross 282
Amie Murphy 282
Faye McColgan 283
Lauren Sparkes 283

The Poems

MOON KIDS

Mummy, Mummy, can we go to the park?
Then put your outfits on,
or you know what'll happen,
you'll flake and burn,
and your bodies will scorch in the sun.

The children got dressed and walked out the door,
leaving the darkness behind.
The suit was dark grey and the face was all black,
almost as though they were blind.

They swung on the swings and slid on the slide.
The roundabout they climbed upon,
spending the rest of their lives in suits,
wondering where their childhood's had gone.

Returning home people laughed at them,
as the moon kids both walked by.
They looked at their mum in cries of despair,
and asked their mummy, why?

They unlocked the front door and strolled into their house,
worn out and tired from the day,
looking around the pitch-black room,
not knowing what to say.

They were tucked into bed and kissed goodnight,
their sad and lonely eyes shut tight,
dreaming of being freed from the dark,
knowing it'll be the same tomorrow night.

Carly Maunsell (13)

I WISH I WERE . . .

I wish I were a seagull and could glide over the sea.
I wish I were a giraffe and could see above the trees.
I wish I were a spider and could catch my prey in my web.
I wish I were a worm and could tunnel deep into the earth.
I wish I were an astronaut and could seek out other worlds.
I wish I were a top class footballer and could play alongside
David Beckham.
I wish I were a pilot and could fly high above the clouds.
I wish I were an explorer and could explore the tropical rainforests.
I wish I were a king and could have servants bring me food.
I wish I were an opera singer and could break the windows in the
Royal Albert Hall.
I wish I were a flower and could brighten up a garden.

I wish I were an inventor and could invent a contraption for
doing your homework for you,
I wish I were a poet and could write some hilarious verses.
I wish I were a millionaire and could give money to people who need it.

I wish I were a peacemaker and could stop all the wars in the world.
I wish I were a designer and could make some trendy gear.
I wish I were able to be happy all the time and never to be made sad.

Michael Palmer (12)
Bexley Grammar School

I WISH . . .

I wish that I could fly without wings,
and view the world's four corners.
I wish I could breathe under the surface of seas,
and dive with the creatures below.

I wish I lived in a house of diamond,
which glistens off the walls.
I wish I could hold the world in my hand,
and could live a perfect life.

I wish that I was filthy rich,
with all the money in the world,
and I wish I caught not one disease,
and live life without a worry.

William Attard (11)
Bexley Grammar School

ONE DAY

Sitting in the classroom
We've got a test today.
I'm wondering, I'm wondering
Will I get an A?
The sheets are given out
The questions look so hard.
If you get an A,
You are given a card.
Sitting in the classroom
The others look so cool.
I wish I had a mirror,
I bet I look a fool.
That's it, it's done,
And yes I've done my best.
Then we get the envelopes.
I look at all the rest.
I know I'm flushing scarlet.
The teacher looks my way.
I open up my envelope,
And find I've got an A.

That's it.
My first ever A.
I cannot wait to get home.
Hooray!

Kelsey Williams (11)
Bexley Grammar School

I Wish I Was A Famous Person

I wish that I was a famous magician who could do tricks all day.
I wish that I was a famous goalkeeper who kept out every shot.
I wish that I was a famous cricketer who scored lots of runs.
I wish that I was a famous tennis player who served lots of aces.
I wish that I was a famous striker who scored the winning goal.
I wish that I was a famous rugby player who scored lots of tries.
I wish that I was a famous athlete who won lots of medals.
I wish that I was a famous inventor who invented a cure for all
                                                    diseases.
I wish that I was a famous steam train driver who built a train that
                                        broke the world steam record.
I wish that I was a famous world leader who brought peace to
                                                    the world.
I wish that I was a famous astronaut and to be the first person to
                                                    land on Mars.
I wish that I was a famous preacher so that I could tell everyone about
                                                    God and Jesus.

Joshua Clipsham (11)
Bexley Grammar School

Dream

I look forward to going to bed
So many thoughts running through my head.
My favourite rhyme drumming in my mind,
but then I find,
I'm in a castle with turrets as tall as the sky.
Shall I be daring, or shall I be shy?
But then it all goes away.
I hear my alarm and I'm filled with fury,
and before I know, I'm dressed and ready to go.

Charlotte Newton (11)
Bexley Grammar School

I MUST BE DREAMING

I must be dreaming,
One time sitting on a chair,
The next sitting in the middle of nowhere,
There is only one reason for it,
I must be dreaming.

Sliding around on the smooth,
Everlasting surface,
Looking over the edge,
A sight even when a baby,
I never even thought of.

I slide too far out,
I am hanging,
My hands slip and I'm falling,
I'm falling, then I open my eyes . . .
I was dreaming.

Monica Kalinska-Bialek (13)
Bexley Grammar School

MY LAND OF PARADISE

My land of Paradise is a place with raspberry oceans,
Pink and purple clouds and chocolate cream potions,
Tangy strawberry rivers running through the mountains,
Blue and green water shooting from the fountains.
Circular shaped squirrels floating in the air,
Bright faced people with vanilla in their hair.
Rainbow coloured disco lights flashing in the sky,
Blood-red killer bees always passing by.
Yellow and black statues blocked in cubes of ice,
Come and visit my Paradise, it is very nice.

Nathan Aspell (11)
Bexley Grammar School

TROUBLE

Every time I get in trouble,
I look back across my life,
At every bad thing I did,
And never did I find a time that trouble paid.

I look at all the times I lost my temper,
When I got into a fight,
And hit people with all my might,
And did it pay? *No!*

All the times I hit my little brother and got grounded.
All the times I was rude to other people older than me
And got pounded,
And did it pay? *No!*

It is hard not to hit little ones when they get on your nerves,
Or not be rude to older ones when they pick on you.
But it doesn't pay,
And trouble is not good
So don't make trouble.

Damilola Bajomo (11)
Bexley Grammar School

DINOSAURS

Dinosaurs are such mythical creatures,
with such detailed features.

They once ruled the Earth,
and you can still find them under some turf.

Their scaly skin
is strong as tin.

And those sharp gnashers,
each one like a dagger.

Look at the size of them, massive and fat,
that would have squashed your house flat.

If they were alive today,
you'd certainly be their number one prey.

Calvin Woodroffe (11)
Bexley Grammar School

I MUST BE DREAMING

I must be dreaming.

I wake up and look around to find a cushion the size of a king-size bed,
The dining table's wood as rough as the spikes on a hedgehog,
And the sofa as big as an aeroplane to fit one thousand people.

I must be dreaming.

I walk to the kitchen to find knives the size of me,
The light bulb as spacious as twenty people stacked on top of
each other,
And the gigantic breakfast chairs as enormous as a huge mansion.

I must be dreaming.

When I woke up I saw everything one hundred times as big as myself,
It was amazing to be like a doll in a tiny doll's house,
I felt so small and afraid.

I *must* have been dreaming.

Monica Patel (12)
Bexley Grammar School

In A Dream

I woke up, rubbed my eyes, and looked around,
Everything was huge,
Twenty times bigger than it was before.
I was in a dream
Where the hole in the cushion which seemed the size of a pinhead,
Was now more like the size of my hand.
A dream
Where the lace of my shoe,
Was now more like the size of a snake,
And where the TV was now more like a cinema screen,
A super size screen in the corner of the living room.

I was in a dream
Where the teacup I drank out of,
Was now a very good hiding place indeed,
And where the remote control was now a metre long.
A dream
Where even the plug socket was too high
To reach with my fingertips,
And where the brass coloured door handle
Was now about one hundred feet above me.

I was in a dream
Where after a while you begin to wonder
Whether it is a dream you're in,
Or is this how it's going to be forever,
Forever stuck in a world of huge things.
A dream
Where you wake up, rub your eyes, and look around,
Everything's back to normal,
Yes it was a dream I was in.

Cleo Harris (13)
Bexley Grammar School

IMAGINE

Imagine if you are asleep,
Sleeping long and sleeping deep,
Then you wake up suddenly,
And what a sight you do see.

Imagine you are six inches high,
You don't know how, you don't know why,
Everything else is gigantic,
You start to panic, getting frantic.

Imagine on your way to school,
You can't get the bus because you're too small.
What on earth can you do
If nobody has noticed you?

Imagine if you go back to sleep,
Sleeping long and sleeping deep,
You might just wake up suddenly,
With no sight for you to see.

Imagine you're back, you are normal now,
You don't know why, you don't know how.
Was it a dream or was it true?
The deciding of that is up to you!

Lois Wallace (12)
Bexley Grammar School

CAR

Car,
Loud and large.
Speeding guiltily.
If only I were seventeen.

Lewis Anderson (11)
Bexley Grammar School

A GARDEN'S NOT SUCHA BEAUTIFUL THING

I galloped onto thick blazes of green
Trapped,
Locked,
How did I get here?
Why, was I here?
All these questions igniting inside my head.
Have these questions got an answer?
I tried and tried to escape.
I felt suffocated, by dashing colours of green staring down at me,
as if I were a peasant.
If only there was a horse or a bird planted in my body
I could leap to safety or fly to freedom.

An ant?
No! It couldn't be.
How could an ant be a size of an elephant that had just had its dinner?
My first reaction was to run as fast as I could, like a cheetah that
had spotted its prey, and was going to pounce upon it and rip out
its flesh.

I ran!
I was knocked down!
I was hurt!
I picked out a sharp blade of grass and poked this *thing.*
It galloped, it leapt, it pounced and it jolted through anything that
got in its way.
Yes! Free, free from blades of grass that were sharp enough to soar
through my diminutive body.
I saw the pleasant sky, it was as blue as waves crashing into cliffs
and the fluffy, bouncy clouds were drifting at ease into the far,
far . . . distance.

An earthquake? No, it couldn't be?
It was as if dinosaur footsteps were thumping the ground and knocking
on my heart.
A huge, bulky shadow darkening my world was coming closer,
and . . . closer.
Here we go again!

Inderveer Singh Salh (12)
Bexley Grammar School

DEAD OR ALIVE!

I opened my eyes,
Am I awake,
I can see,
But can it be,
A bird as big as a tree.

The grass is tall,
Or am I small,
I call and call.

But no one can hear,
For I fear,

That I shall die,
And birds shall fly,

And pick my bones clean,
Until they shine and start to gleam.

Darkness is here,
Darkness is there,
Darkness is nearly everywhere,

Am I alive,
Or am I not? . . .

Jean-Paul Mascarenhas (12)
Bexley Grammar School

I MUST BE DREAMING

I had this weird feeling
I felt very small
I must be dreaming.

I woke up in my green bed
It looked like a vast field
I must be dreaming.

My cushion was an enormous white cloud
Standing on the field
I must be dreaming.

I slapped myself
To wake myself up I told myself
I must be dreaming.

But nothing happened
I must be awake
Oh *No!* I'm not *dreaming.*

Ian Witsey (130
Bexley Grammar School

A SHARK

A shark,
Ferocious and deadly,
Swimming sneakily,
As though it was the smooth,
sleek water itself.
If only I was a fly on the wall!

Sarah Wildblood (11)
Bexley Grammar School

I MUST BE DREAMING

I must be dreaming
I never knew grass was so elephantine
I never knew how petrifying insects are
they go at rapid speeds,
as fast as the speed of light,
they give me chills and frights.
I must be dreaming,
the sun isn't gleaming,
I see a twig, it's the size of a tree,
three times bigger than me.
I must be dreaming,
in the distance I see a mountainous rock,
with a kitten the size of a tiger on it,
can I be sleeping?
I must be dreaming . . .

Jake Gowers (12)
Bexley Grammar School

WHAT I SAW AS I OPENED MY EYES

As I opened my eyes I saw,
Trees one hundred feet tall,
A land where nothing is small,
An ant the size of my hand,
Giant footprints in the sand.
As I opened my eyes I saw,
A dolphin leaping, fifty feet long,
A magnificent bird, cawing in song.
Giant children having fun,
The huge and golden setting sun.
I opened my eyes and saw,
A dream.

Matthew Jenkins (12)
Bexley Grammar School

THE JUNGLE

I opened my eyes,
And I saw, I saw,
A jungle,
But this looked like my garden,
Only magnified a thousand times,
My own blades of grass,
Are larger than me,
Oh! But what is this
This thing,
Which makes the hairs on the back of my neck
stand up?
It's a monster charging at me,
It's making an irritating noise,
It's getting louder, louder, louder,
It's coming closer, and I see it,
The silhouette is lighting up,
The monster is a bee,
But it looks like a monster to me.
It's coming towards me,
I close my eyes,
But nothing is happening,
Oh! The anxiety,
It's killing me,
I open my eyes,
Everything's normal again,
I think it was a dream,
Was it a dream or not . .?

Charnpreet Minhas (12)
Bexley Grammar School

I MUST BE DREAMING

I wake up,
Everything is gigantic,
My pillow is now rough,
I must be dreaming.

I climb down the bed,
The door is so big.
I slip through the crack,
I must be dreaming.

I go down the stairs,
The TV is huge.
I can't reach the sofa,
I must be dreaming.

I need a drink,
I'm too small for the cup.
I'll have to stay thirsty,
I must be dreaming.

I need some food,
Even the food is too big!
I'll have to stay hungry,
I must be dreaming.

Oh no! It's the cat!
What shall I do?
I'll have to hide,
I must be dreaming.

I go back upstairs,
Climb up the bed.
I go back to sleep,
I was dreaming.

Lauren Bartlett (12)
Bexley Grammar School

SMALL

I woke up and saw a huge lamp on
a large table across the room.

I woke up to find a giant cat
purring in the corner.

I woke up and found a car parked
on the floor big enough to drive.

I woke up and looked out the window
to find an enormous tree
with a branch the size of ten.

I woke up to find a big person
walking up the path.

I woke up and saw a house twice
its usual size.

I had shrunk.

Ben Church (12)
Bexley Grammar School

THIS IS JUST TO SAY . . .

I'm sorry for
Winding you up
And teasing when
You're unwell.

But I got some
Fun out of it
And I bet you
Did as well.

Daniel Jones (11)
Bexley Grammar School

I Wish I Lived . . .

I wish I lived at the bottom of the ocean with the fish at my command,
I wish I lived in the depths of space with the world at my command,
I wish I lived in a palace with servants and riches at my command,
I wish I lived in the centre of a diamond with its glory at my command,
I wish I lived in a cosy cottage with the view at my command,
I wish I lived where I do now with my family's love at my command,
I wish I lived in a place where there was non-stop fun at my command,
I wish I lived in a place where there was endless time at my command,
I wish I lived in a world where there was happiness at my command,
I wish I lived in a time where there was no suffering at my command,
I wish I lived in a house where there was silence at my command,
I'm glad I live with my family but they are not at my command!

Anthony Macina (11)
Bexley Grammar School

I Must Be Dreaming

I must be dreaming I was lying on my bed,
Now I am lost on a desert of quilt covers,
Before they were all soft and smooth,
Now they are all rough and dirty,
My pillows are as big as a king-sized bed.
I must be dreaming,
I am standing on my bedside table,
It is so rough and splintering,
Before it was so rough and shiny.
I must be dreaming,
A giant roaring monster is lurking on the landing,
Then I realise it's not a monster after all,
It is a furry, fluffy tabby cat,
Then I wake up and it was a dream after all.

Daniel Wendon (12)
Bexley Grammar School

WHAT'S HAPPENING?

What's happening?
I wake up from my nap,
What's happening?
The whole room has enlarged five times!
What's happening?
Or is it me that has shrunk?

That's weird!
The carpet looks like the sea,
That's weird!
The settee looks like a cliff.
That's weird!
My sister and parents are like giants to me.

Boom! Boom!
The TV shouts at me,
Purr! Purr!
The cat shakes the floor.
Ring! Ring!
Oh no! I think the world is going to end!

Joseph Tinlin (12)
Bexley Grammar School

THE SUN

Red and yellow
Shining brightly
Like a dancing flame
I wish the sun would
Come out today!

Chantelle Simper (11)
Bexley Grammar School

FINAL TEAR

It happens all too suddenly,
When you're least aware.
Time drifts by immediately,
For those you love and care.

Nobody understands the pain,
That loss can provide,
Because all you do is in vain,
For those at your side.

It is hard to have to part,
Your sadness is too great.
But you have to find within your heart,
That this is their fate.

But soon you will stop,
You'll have realised your fear.
Because you now have reached the top,
You have cried your final tear.

Jennifer Hien (11)
Bexley Grammar School

I'M SORRY

I have eaten the chocolates,
That were under your pillow,
Which you were probably going to
Have as a midnight feast.
I'm ever so sorry, please forgive me,
But I've also got your
New CD!

George Unitt (12)
Bexley Grammar School

A SMALL DAY

Ah what a wonderful dream,
It would be great to be bigger than everything,
I would crush the school, damn it,
Oh,
This is bad.
The floor of my room looks like an unforgiving sea
So far away.
This time I'm the small one.
A thought struck me.
Lucky, Lucky, Lucky
Lucky, Lucky, Lucky
The family dog.
I jumped onto a soft patch of carpet,
I bounced onto a pillow,
Luckily
Lucky, Lucky, Lucky
Lucky, Lucky, Lucky.
I moved on down the hall, an abyss of doom
I swerved from my clumsy sister's foot,
The foot the size of a table,
Clambering down the stairs, with difficulty,
Gazing at a far off mountain, a bowl
Lucky, Lucky, Lucky
Lucky, Lucky, Lucky
A call from my mother.
A sound of an aeroplane taking off from nearby.
A bark like a thunderclap,
Lucky, Lucky, Lucky
Lucky, Lucky, Lucky
A bite so much worse than that bark,
Definitely.

Philip Bayley (12)
Bexley Grammar School

LARGER THAN LIFE

I took a step further
And a hole punch was there,
I dashed,
I jumped,
And I ran out of the way,
Just in time as it was pushed down.

I took a step further,
And two trunks with feet on the end were there.
I realised then that it was a person,
I ran for my life as he took a step,
I rolled,
I dived,
I sprinted,
And climbed,
As the giant walked straight past me.
My heart was pounding,
About to explode,
Yet so many questions were running through me;
Where am I?
What is this place?
I took a step further and a beast was before me.
I leapt,
I galloped,
I pounced,
And I sprang.
But it was no use,
The horse fell upon me,
Upon me it fell,
And I was me no longer.

Daniel Burns (13)
Bexley Grammar School

I WISH I'D WON . . .

I wish I'd won a gold medal for gymnastics.
I wish I'd won the running race on Sports Day.
I wish I'd won a trophy at the championships.
I wish I'd won the lottery on Saturday night.
I wish I'd won a flash sports car glittering in the sun.
I wish I'd won a holiday where it's warm and peaceful.
I wish I'd won a country home to sit and relax in the summer.
I wish I'd won the handstand competition at gym club.
I wish I'd won a television so I could sit and watch programmes.
I wish I'd won a DVD player to keep down our caravan.
I wish I'd won a CD Walkman so I can listen to my favourite tunes.
I wish I'd won this poetry competition.

Lara Williams (11)
Bexley Grammar School

I WISH

I wish I lived on the moon,
away from the everyday hustle and bustle.
I wish I lived under the sea,
with beautiful sea creatures' company.
I wish I lived in the Arctic,
with the soft, fluffy polar bears.
I wish I lived in the clouds,
with angels as my friends.
I wish I lived on a beach,
with the sun beaming down all day long.
I wish I lived in a jungle,
and lived a crazy jungle life,
But most of all I wish I lived where I do,
with human people as my company.

Harriet Coombs (11)
Bexley Grammar School

I WISH I WAS

I wish I was a polar bear,
never getting cold in the warm coat of fur.
I wish I was a great white shark,
living in the deep blue sea.
I wish I was a furry hamster,
storing precious food.
I wish I was a baby monkey,
swinging tree to tree.
I wish I was a basilisk,
walking on the silver water.
I wish I was a flying frog,
leaping through the air.
I wish I was the atlas moth,
with beautiful wings.
I wish I was the chameleon,
Changing bright unusual colours.
I wish I was a cheetah,
running furiously through the jungle.
Most of all I wish I was me!

Faye Highland (11)
Bexley Grammar School

A GRAMMAR POEM

Knight
Brave and bold
Fighting fearlessly
Like a wild beast
If only knights never die.

Amanda Ly (11)
Bexley Grammar School

I WISH...

I wish I could go to Florida to swim with dolphins.
I wish I could own a necklace with special charms from
                                            all over the world.
I wish I could spend a day in the sky,
walking on fluffy clouds and sleeping on the shining stars.
I wish I could own an animal from each country.
I wish I could have a beautiful garden with an archway
of flowers and peaceful wind chimes ringing all day.
I wish I could have a top made from the softest material in the world.
I wish I could swim in the peaceful, deep blue coral reef.
I wish I could swim in the sea through the coral and starfish
amongst the dolphins and the brightly coloured fish.
I wish I could see the sunset, the flame colours shining brightly
above a white snow carpet.
I wish I could have a bracelet of delicate flowers that could never break.
I wish I could visit the beach every day and walk through the soft
golden sand and hear the gentle call of the sea.
I wish I could visit the rainforest and taste the tropical fruits.

Alexandra Tolfree (11)
Bexley Grammar School

GRAMMAR POEM

Cheetah
Spotty and yellow
Running fast
Like a bullet
If only there were more of them.

Samantha Cefai (11)
Bexley Grammar School

I WISH

I wish I were an alien zooming through space.
I wish I were an opera singer getting much applause.
I wish I lived at the top of the leaning tower of Pisa,
getting so many praises.
I wish I were a shimmering king being adored wherever I go.
I wish I weighed ten thousand fold, the strongest man in the world.
I wish I were the wisest man in the world, everyone would come from
all around the world, to ask me wise questions.
I wish I lived in a humongous mansion, with 50,00000000000 servants.
I wish I were in a silver submarine, exploring the seven seas.
I wish I were a treasured chicken, laying golden Easter eggs
                                        for everyone.
I wish I lived on Easter Island with the Easter bunny eating eggs in
and out of Easter.
I wish I was the richest man in the world owning
£9999999999999999999999999999999999999999 and 9/ninths.
I wish I was five inches and lived in a golden shoe.

Tolu Elebiju (11)
Bexley Grammar School

THIS IS JUST TO SAY . . .

I am sorry
for breaking your lamp,
your lovely lamp.
That's blue, red and green.
Lamp that we all love so much.
I will replace it with another one,
much better than that.

Emily Downs (11)
Bexley Grammar School

I WISH...

I wish I lived on a paradise island, with a golden beach
and a dozen diamond studded mansions,
a swimming pool the size of three lakes and a safari park.
I wish I could teleport to a land of chocolate whenever I wanted,
and when I go there I could eat anything I wanted without it
                                                    making my teeth rot.
I wish I lived in a world with no war or poverty and everyone got
on with each other, where there were no need for prisons or courts,
where there was no corruption, where there were no wealthy people
but no deprived people either.
I wish I had a bedroom where whenever my mum told me to tidy
my room it did it itself, and I had a robot that did all my clothes for me.
I wish I knew everything and whenever I did a test, I always got all
the answers right and always got As.
I wish I was the best at all the sports and everyone envied me.

Gurdeep Briah (11)
Bexley Grammar School

I WISH...

I wish I was an astronaut floating up in space.
I wish I were on TV earning lots of money.
I wish I were a bird so I could fly across the sky.
I wish I were a teacher telling off all the children.
I wish I were a witch casting lots of spells.
I wish I could eat McDonald's every day of the year.
I wish I had a pet penguin living in my room.
I wish I had my own country mansion with grounds
And views as well.
I wish I could win the Olympics swimming.
I wish I could visit Disneyland every day of the year.
I wish I could swap bodies with someone for a day.

Ella Gardiner (12)
Bexley Grammar School

BACK IN TIME

I wish I lived in the years of World War II, to be an evacuee.
I wish I lived in Victorian England, to meet the author Charles Dickens.
I wish I lived in Tudor times, to fight in the infamous War of the Roses.
I wish I lived in Middle Ages, to see the disease plague spread like
wildfire.
I wish I lived in 1066, to be a soldier for the victorious Normans.
I wish I lived in Rome, the city of luxury, in Roman times.
I wish I lived on a Viking boat, always having adventures.
I wish I lived in the Iron Age, to be a simple farmer.
I wish I lived in Ancient Egypt, the land of curses and hieroglyphics.
I wish I lived in 3200BC, to be one of the builders of Stonehenge.
I wish I lived in the years after the Ice Age to try and find the Irish Elk.
I wish I lived when the dinosaurs were alive, then I would take photos
and evidence back.

Connor Gorrard-Smith (11)
Bexley Grammar School

I WISH . . .

I wish I was a dolphin swimming alongside boats of enthralled tourists.
I wish I was a cat, sprawled lazily in the sunshine.
I wish I was a bird, cosy in my little nest that I made myself.
I wish I was a dog, running after a ball I was longing to chew.
I wish I was a horse, galloping through the grass at full speed.
I wish I was a squirrel, watching as children rolled nuts at me for
my lunch.
I wish I was a rabbit, coming out of my burrow at twilight to feed.
I wish I was a lamb, frisking about in the field that was my home.
I wish I was a duck, searching my pond for food with my tail in the air.
I wish I was a mouse, sleeping in my little nest of bits and pieces.

Sonita Baker (11)
Bexley Grammar School

I WISH I LIVED . . .

I wish I lived in a Pharaoh's tomb in Egypt.
I wish I lived in a chocolate house with sweets and marshmallows
around the sides.
I wish I lived in a palace with diamonds and jewels.
I wish I lived in a cottage with fireplaces and a farm.
I wish I lived in space with my own pet alien.
I wish I lived a normal and peaceful life in the country.
I wish I lived with furry cats, dogs and hamsters.
I wish I lived with all of my family.
I wish I lived in a country estate.
I wish I lived in a golden palace, where everyone comes to visit me and
brings me gifts.
I wish I lived somewhere where it never rains.
I wish I lived in Florida with sand as gold as the sun and sea as blue
as the skies.
I wish I lived on a fluffy cloud in the sky.
I wish I lived with all of my friends.
I wish I lived with my head full of knowledge.
I wish I lived in places where there were parties all the time.
I wish I lived . . .

Stacey Phipps (11)
Bexley Grammar School

SMOKE

Smoke
Thick, heavy
Expanding quickly
As suffocating as a plastic bag
If only the world could get rid of it.

Sam Fisher (11)
Bexley Grammar School

I WISH POEM

I wish I lived on a gleaming gold island,
Where I could swim with dolphins and own my own two acre football
                                                                pitch.
I wish that I had my very own coral reef.
I wish I had over five houses to own to have on my island,
So if I wanted to be alone I had five choices to go.
I wish I had loads of slaves and butlers,
So I would not have to do everything myself.
I wish my island was made of gold and riches,
That means my island will be known to the world.
I wish I would be so happy on this island,
Then I would lead a happy life.

Charlie Tennent (12)
Bexley Grammar School

THE SHARK

Sleek, smooth gliding through the water,
Flying like a plane,
Scouring the ocean for prey.

Enormous teeth for devouring its catch,
A colossal mouth to swallow anything,
Tail for speed and
Fins for steering through the water.

Casting fear in all that sees it,
Fish darting for any shelter they can.
This lived 12,000 years ago,
And it's a shame we can't see it today.

Joe Simpson (11)
Bexley Grammar School

I WISH...

I wish I were playing football at the new
Wembley Stadium in the sunshine.

I wish I were playing rugby
on the wet mud at the park.

I wish I were playing basketball in the sports hall,
jumping towards the hoop.

I wish I were skating in the blistering cold
on thick ice.

I wish I were having a world tour,
sailing across the seas.

I wish I were snowboarding in the snow.

Jeff Riza (12)
Bexley Grammar School

GRAMMAR POEM

Cappuccino
Hot and frothy
Steaming furiously
Like a kettle
If only it was mine.

Duck
Feathery and soft
Quacking continuously
Like a car honking
If only it was on my plate.

Daniel Sydee (11)
Bexley Grammar School

LIGHTNING

Fast and bright
Glowing quickly
Like a fire
If only it couldn't hurt you.

Hanaa Neetoo (11)
Bexley Grammar School

OGRE

Ogre,
Large and ugly,
Storming thunderously,
Like a heavy tree falling,
If only creatures like this were real.

Daniel Burn Webster (11)
Bexley Grammar School

FOOTBALL

Football
Large and inflated
Zooming horribly
Like a dragon
If only I could kick the thing.

Philip Gosling (11)
Bexley Grammar School

LIFE OF THE POET

Poem, poem, what will they think up next?
With the clever and rhyming text.

Set in paragraphs, they're read again and again,
You can imagine poets, refilling their pen.

Some Poet Laureate of their age,
Their feather or quill blotting ink on the page.

So may these poems last forever,
Written with the author's endeavour.

Thomas Hart (11)
Bexley Grammar School

THIS IS JUST TO SAY . . .

I have taken
the car keys
and driven the car
round the block.

Which you will
probably need
to take
to work.

But I forgot
I am only eleven
and I found
a driver's licence.

Peter Willson (11)
Bexley Grammar School

GRAMMAR POEM

Dolphin
Happy and playful
Diving smoothly
Like a glorious wave
If only I were one.

Sophie Haslam (11)
Bexley Grammar School

CANDLES

Warm and mesmerising
Shining brightly
Like a sun in the sky
If only it would never end.

Samuel Ly (11)
Bexley Grammar School

GRAMMAR POEMS

Cheetah
Spotty and so yellow
Running thunderously
Like rain tumbling
As fast as the wind
If only I had a pet cheetah, Aaaaaaaagh!

Amit Bhanderi (11)
Bexley Grammar School

COFFEE EYES

For a moment, just imagine,
Hypothetically speaking,
I told you I loved you . . .
What would you do?
Would you laugh, and walk away?
Then tomorrow we'll realise our fragile universe was too small.
For just one loving heart.
Would you stay, and stare?
The stained glass silence too loud to bear,
Coffee eyes fall,
As our universe breaks apart.

It's OK, I won't cry,
Here, so you can tell yourself I'm fine.
I'll hide,
The heartbreak hyperbole, just real enough to hurt,
And you can tell yourself I'm fine.

What if I told you,
Hypothetically speaking,
I'd loved you since the day you first said my name,
One year, six days, still counting.

You'll turn around then, and look at me with,
Coffee eyes and smile,
And say you feel the same,
And our universe is safe,
And you'll hold my hand,
Then everyone will know I'm yours,
For the keeping.

Hypothetically speaking,
Of course.

Clare Allen (15)
Charles Darwin School

CLEW BAY, WESTPORT-EIRE

As I look across the ocean,
I cry a thousand tears,
Each one placed so carefully,
Throughout the million years.
The coldness of the water,
Makes me gasp with awe,
I move towards the horizon,
My worries I feel no more.

The beauty of the mountains,
Behind me, rise above so high,
Destruction, war and killing,
All this makes me wonder why.
The clouds, they fly so freely,
Swaying with the wind,
I ask God to forgive me,
For all that I have sinned.

To completely be at one,
With yourself is just the best,
I float upon this feeling,
With which I must caress.
I pity all those people,
Who have nowhere to themselves,
They must find somewhere to think, to pray,
Into their spirits, must inwardly delve.

Stephanie O'Brien (13)
Charles Darwin School

MY FAMILY

My mum thinks she is so cool
Her name is Mary-Sue
She's so embarrassing when I'm at school
She thinks she's twenty-two!

My dad is a builder
Whenever he finishes a job
He thinks he should be called 'Sir'
Although his real name is Bob.

My sister is called Rosalie
And one day when I was in bed
She was so mean to me
She poured water on my head!

My nan and grandpa have twelve cats
We call all twelve 'Dude'
They also have a dog and two rats
It costs them a fortune in food.

My uncle is called James
He is ever so nice
He's got so many board games,
But he's lost all the dice.

Rachel Schafer (12)
Charles Darwin School

THE MAKING OF A POEM

The young poet sits down and casts for ideas.
He thinks new and fresh thoughts, but nothing seems clear.
Firstly he considers the comedy side,
but too many jokes, may bring a sigh.

He stares into space, with his eyes opened wide.
He wonders again, as the planes fly by.
Should I keep it true, or should it be a lie?
But a glimmer of hope, soon will decide.

His pen writes as fast, as a bobsleigh on ice.
His new and fresh thoughts were coming to life.
He extends his vocabulary and tries to impress,
but only time, will decide his prospects.

He is nearly there, but can't quite find,
the way to end this fabricated rhyme.
At first he reflects on a happy conclusion,
he must think of something, and make his decision!

At last, the poem has reached the end,
the final stanza is complete.
The poet looks back at his detailed work,
to check if everything is correct and neat.

Daniel Slade (13)
Charles Darwin School

THE WINTER WIND

Carelessly, swiftly rushes along,
The harsh and devious winter wind,
That quietly sings it's signalling song,
To show that it has come.

As you see this terrible wind,
His great thin face turns into a grin,
He uses hundreds of razor-sharp knives,
To make sure that he is determined to win
Control of you and your surrounding.

As animals run for shelter in holes by the river,
The bare trees nearby just stand there and shiver,
Wincing with pain from his cold,
And being beaten into a permanent mould.

The rushing wind gradually picks up,
To release the last of its energy galore,
Life starts to breathe again,
And the cold, harsh wind is gone once more.

Stephen Peneycad (13)
Charles Darwin School

ZODIAC

Twinkle, twinkle little stars,
        Astrologers search so far.
Up above the Milky Way,
        Zodiac signs to show the way.
Always wanting more and more,
        Leo lion with a roar.

Twinkle, twinkle Gemini,
    Many people think they lie.
Aries, Pisces, Capricorn,
    All depends on when you're born.
Libra, Taurus and the rest,
    Who's to say that they're the best?

Claire Archer (12)
Christ Church CE High School

THE ZODIAC

The sky, big, black and empty at times;
The zodiac is formed,
Through simple
but meaningful signs.

An imaginary belt of heavens,
The apparent path of the sun,
moon and principal planets.
All twelve signs of the
Zodiac are in the sky.

Many people follow the zodiac every day to live their lives,
as they read their horoscopes in the news.

People believe that the zodiac sign of their birth month
will tell them what to do and what to say
every moment of their day.

Believing that if following their advice under their sign
will help from taking a chance of getting the blues.

Lee Fishlock (12)
Christ Church CE High School

ZODIAC POEM

Aries the ram is where I'll begin,
From March to April is where it fits in.
Taurus seems to nicely follow,
April to May that's not to hard to swallow.
Gemini always stays as a pair,
May to June each other always there.
Cancer the crab could give a bit of a nip,
From June to July I'll move on real quick.
Leo the lion (that's my sign you know),
From July to August what a wonderful flow.
Virgo I think seems a little bit mystic,
From August to September, boy I'm glad I missed it.
Libra wants to weigh up the odds,
From September to October bet they collect bits and bobs.
Scorpio like a scorpion can be pretty snappy,
From October to November I'm sure they'll be happy.
Sagittarius looks a bit half and half,
From November to December they're good for a laugh.
Capricorn looks like they could be a mixed bunch,
From December to January they'll have plenty to munch.
Aquarius perhaps keeps their affections flowing,
From January to February they'll be completely mind-blowing.
Pisces a pair of fish is where I'll end my poem,
From February to March, that's all, bye-bye,
Must be going!

Mathew Tippett (11)
Christ Church CE High School

STARS

The stars are glaring in my face,
Millions of them from out of space.
Virgo, Aries, all from afar
A virgin, a ram behind the stars.

Gemini, Capricorn and many more,
I wonder who they're all for?
My hair is crawling along my face,
As I wonder what is happening in outer space.

Hannah Verlinden (11)
Christ Church CE High School

A ZODIAC POEM

Leo lion is a star in the sky,
it glitters like the gem of your eye.
Cancer crab swims in the sea
eating as he goes as happy as can be.
Pisces fish is swimming along,
keeping his eyes out for sharks big and strong.
Capricorn the goat looks around for edible coats.
Sagittarius pulls his bow back with strength,
the arrow soars through the air at an amazing length.
Taurus the bull tries to get the red cloth,
but away from the bull the cloth is pulled.
Gemini the twins fight over the rattle with
kicks and screams and whinges they battle.
Wrong, right, heavy or light the Libra scales cry.
Virgo virgin clean and bright
wears a long robe as pure as white.
Scorpio scorpion a creature to fear
beware of that sting if you dare go near.
Aries the ram with big curly horns
wanders over to a field and walks over some corn.
Water bearer carrying high life giving water from the sky,
Aquarius one of the zodiac signs could be a birthday,
Yours or mine.

Karen Thatcher (11)
Christ Church CE High School

THE ZODIAC POEM

In China there is a belief,
That there is a zodiac of animals.
They come out when darkness falls.
It is a good thing to believe.
They rule the stars,
And can be seen from the streets,
As well as cars.
The thudding stops of rushing feet.
There is a creature running,
It looks brave and cunning.
It leaps over the scorpion
It's Leo the lion!

Kayleigh Offen (11)
Christ Church CE High School

CANCER THE CRAB

Has an amazing amount of flab,
and he passes by,
during June and July,
his shell is so plain,
and it's got to his brain,
that he's the most boring star sign of all,
being so small, he feels like a fool
and he hides away in the sky.

Howard Cockram (11)
Christ Church CE High School

ZODIAC POEM

My star sign is Leo,
A lion in the sky,
Waiting to pounce on its prey,
not day, but night,
then he cleans his long brown coating,
he hunts down Aries the ram,
and eats his prey on his own,
and as he gets tired,
Leo the lion goes to sleep,
to rest his useless bones,
and can't wait to feast another night.

Barry Fannon (11)
Christ Church CE High School

ONCE THERE WAS LEO

Once there was Leo, a lion in the sky,
The stars twinkled like a diamond in his eye.
Along came Scorpio running across the sky,
He ran so fast it looked like he could fly.
Leo the lion said goodbye,
Then he ran halfway across the sky.
Poor Leo sat down and said
'Why do I have to live with the sky as my bed?'

Marie Brough (11)
Christ Church CE High School

STARS AND THEIR LIVES

There once was a lion,
A lion called Leo,
Who had a pet monkey,
Called Cleo.

That brings me to Pisces,
A talented fish,
With lemon and limes,
What a tasty dish.

There once was a woman
Called Aquarius,
With her boyfriend,
Called Sagittarius.

Taurus is a mighty bull,
And hated anything red,
He tried to headbutt all of them,
But ended up in bed.

There once was a Virgo,
That liked to walk,
She couldn't go on her own,
Because she liked to talk.

There once was a crab,
A crab called Cancer.
He was a very nice crab,
And an excellent dancer.

That's it from me and my riddles,
About the stars.
I have one last question,
Are girls from Venus, Jupiter or Mars?

Lucy Kingsnorth (11)
Christ Church CE High School

ZODIAC SIGN

Leo the lion leaps and roars,
Kills his prey with his big sharp claws.
Scorpio has a big sharp sting,
And he's not scared of anything.

Capricorn the goat has great big horns,
And he has got a look of brawn.
Gemini are the twins,
But they are good, they do no sins.

Taurus the bull snuffles and snorts,
Not looking nice his face is contort.
Cancer the crab snaps with his pincers,
But touches wood and never gets splinters.

Sagittarius takes his shot,
But he misses the target quite a lot.
Pisces the fish gurgles and swims,
He is the best because he has fins.

Aries the ram grunts and charges,
He is mean but he's not the largest.
Libra is scales weighing up and down,
But people look down at their weight and frown.

Aquarius is a person carrying water,
But they could do with getting a little shorter.
Virgo the maiden cooks the food,
But she always gets in a mood.

Paul Barford (12)
Christ Church CE High School

ZODIAC

As the stars sparkle in the night sky,
The UFOs go for a fly.

The people look in a dazzled stare,
The kids all shout this is fair!

All the adults stare without saying a word,
They roam through the air like a herd.

The stars disappear behind the clouds,
The people start to shout real loud.

When the clouds have gone away,
The stars come back from their holiday.

They come out in a weird shape,
It looks like police tape.

It starts to tell a wonderful tale,
But then it starts to hail.

Everyone rushes in out of the storm,
The stars disappear like a burning dorm.

By dawn all the stars have gone,
The people moan for so long!

Clive Chittenden (11)
Christ Church CE High School

A SUDDEN CALM

Walking down the street the rain is pouring down,
Trickling down the windowpanes the wind is howling loud,
Falling leaves swirl round and round,
The trees are rocking fiercely, they make a creaking sound.

People hurrying, rushing to get home,
Some with others and some alone.
Suddenly all is calm, the wind stops howling,
The leaves lie still, the rain has gone,
But in the air, a chill.

Hannah Dring (11)
Dover Grammar School For Girls

LEGS!

Hairy legs are scary legs
With hairs the size of bear's hairs
It's a jungle out there.

Sporty legs are naughty legs
With kicks, snicks and trips
The referee will blow the whistle
And that will be it.

Girlie legs are swirly legs
With socks, frocks and skirts.
Watch out the high heel might
Come in, and kick you where it hurts.

Smooth legs are rude legs
They're shiny and they're sleek
Sometimes they're playful under tables,
Because they tickle your feet.

Buuutttttt . . .

Hairy legs are the scariest legs
You don't know what you'll find,
But in my mind . . .
Hairy legs are the best kind.

Catherine Johnston (12)
Dover Grammar School For Girls

BUTTERFLIES FLUTTERBIES

Butterflies Flutterbies
Was what I used to call them
Butterflies Flutterbies
I used to say, they went into a cocoon.

Butterflies Flutterbies
Fly across the light blue sky
Butterflies Flutterbies
Their beautiful colours catch your eye.

Butterflies Flutterbies
They flutter through your hair
Butterflies Flutterbies
They swing and fling through the air.

Butterflies Flutterbies
I would love to jump and play
Butterflies Flutterbies
Don't worry I will come and play another day.

Elizabeth Pooley (12)
Dover Grammar School For Girls

BOUNCY BALL

Bouncy ball
Bounce on the wall
Bounce up and down
Bounce all around
When I go flat then I'll stop,
But until then
I'll bounce non-stop
I am a bouncy ball.

Caroline Rose (11)
Dover Grammar School For Girls

LOVE, SORROW, HOPE

The pride of the Twin Towers has fallen
made into rubble by hate.

People are screaming and running,
They see sights of destruction.
Enough to want to close their eyes forever.
Dust which makes you suffocate.
Frozen by terror for seconds, minutes, hours.
The horror, impossible to believe.
Why? Who?
Stunned, disgusted.
The innocent are dead, why?
Our world is so small, seen from the stars.
Yet so big and full of people.
We must make our lives on earth together,
Be rid of hate and vengeance.
Let's start again with hope.
Use kind and good words to fight hate.
As the planes crashed and the building fell,
The people's words were 'I love you.'
Let us start from here.

Emily Hazrati (11)
Dover Grammar School For Girls

MIKE

There was a young boy named Mike,
Who really loved to eat Pike.
The freaky fish,
Was his favourite dish,
He ate it while riding his bike.

Ruth Marlow (11)
Dover Grammar School For Girls

PITTA-PATTA

Pitta patta
Pitta-patta
Goes the rain against my window
Softer and softer until
It stops.
Large puddles in the road
Waiting
Wating for what no one knows.
Waiting until
Splash.
Children everywhere
Coloured boots all around
The children go in
The puddle is still once more.
The sun comes out
I look out
But the puddle's gone,
Gone until the next rainfall.

Sophie Gray (11)
Dover Grammar School For Girls

THE WIND

T   hrough the trees he rustles.
H   e rattles the letterbox as he passes.
E   very day he's there, even if he's just a slight breeze.

W   hizzing round the garden.
I   n through all the nooks and crannies.
N   ever stops to take a break.
D   ay after day you'll find him forever carrying on.

Natasha Clinch (11)
Dover Grammar School For Girls

SHOPPING!

I think shopping is extremely great,
I always go with my mate.
I go to buy clothes,
Make-up, sweets and shoes.
I'm in the cinema, take a seat,
I saw one boy and me,
I tried not to cry.
I needed the toilet, *ah!*
I've been!
I took a browse
Nothing to get,
But I still had a great time,
And I spent ten pounds and ninety-nine pence.

Niccy Mounteney (11)
Dover Grammar School For Girls

SUN AND MOON

The sun glows bright,
the moon does at night.
It gives you light
throughout the night.
Eating carrots helps
your eyes work right.
It helps you see,
it helps you and me.
We can talk,
we can walk,
we can sing,
and we know what we are doing.

Amy Collier (11)
Dover Grammar School For Girls

THE DOG

A dog walks by with his tail in the air,
He befriends you and sits on your chair.
Dogs are kind and fluffy,
He was called Muffy.

He does a lot of funny tricks,
And plays along with the farmyard chicks.
In the morning, he licks your face,
Just like a friend in the human race.

Tick, tick, tick, the clock is ticking.
My dog finally stops licking.
Poof, he's gone in the blink of an eye.
When he died, he made me cry.

Chloe Carr (11)
Dover Grammar School For Girls

SITTING BY THE SHORE

I was looking at the sea
Shining with gold.
I was staring at the sun
Turning red.
I was whispering to the seagulls
Don't cry,
And waving to the trees goodbye.

I was listening to the people talking,
And was clapping at the birds for singing.
I was cheering at the actress for dancing.
I was sitting by the shore thinking.

Wahida Islam (11)
Dover Grammar School For Girls

THE BULLY

I cower in the corner,
She's spotted me.
I try to hide but she has the eyes of an eagle.
I flinch, but before she's struck, I feel pain.
The pain of knowing no one cares.
My mother doesn't believe me,
I have no friends to tell.
It hurts. Then she hits.
I feel no pain from that.
Only my heart and soul are damaged.
I hear laughter, and I see her aim again.
I hear a voice similar to mine, shouting at them.
The laughter stops.
They walk away.
I have victory.
I have defeated . . .
. . . the bully.

Lindsay Kennett (12)
Dover Grammar School For Girls

MY DREAM

I dream, a very lovely dream,
About the West End Shows.
It's great dancing in the light
During the evening shine.
Singing in the streets,
Acting in the acts,
Till my dream is through.
Then as I awake
And get myself up,
I find my dream's come true.

Anieka Saxby (11)
Dover Grammar School For Girls

GUESS WHO?

Big brown eyes staring through you,
Drooping down, a mischievous glint.
Huge, silky ears always alert,
A nose the colour of shiny flint.
A protruding tongue lapping up water,
Surrounded by sharp and shiny teeth.
Whiskers stuck up high in the air,
With leathery lips just beneath.
A coat covered with white and tan splodges,
Keeping him warm when it's cold.
Tiny legs that will support him,
When he's young, middle-aged and old.
Paws padding softly around the world,
Accompanied by the sharpest of claws.
Walking around sniffing here and there,
Running everywhere on all fours.
A tail raised high in the air,
In this position is always found.
Wagging softly to and fro,
That's what makes Archie the basset hound.

Charlotte Vines (11)
Dover Grammar School For Girls

SNOWMAN

Crispy snow beneath my feet
Build a snowman, what a treat!
Stars and moon so bright above
Warm blankets, nice and snug.
Lay my head upon my pillow
Sweet dreams I hope will follow.

Wake up I can't wait!
Where's my snowman, am I too late?
Wrap up warm, hat, gloves, two coats,
Rush outside, no time for toast.
Where's my snowman? Where's he gone?
The sun came out and he's moved on.

Emily O'Hare (11)
Dover Grammar School For Girls

A THOUGHT FOR CHRISTMAS

People hurry in busy streets,
Bundled up high with treasure.
Christmas lights all shiny and exciting,
Will we be ready? Never!
Pretty up your houses, deck your rooms
                              in tinsel and holly.
Decorate your trees with red and green,
The smiles of delight can all be seen.
But spare a thought for one and all,
The lonely and the cold.
It's not all happiness with comfort and joy,
Especially if you're old.
Let's make a silent wish right now,
From violent war, bring calming peace.
Stop the suffering in the world,
Think of God this special day at least!
Try to bring some care and feeling,
End your silly little feuds,
Give this Christmas warmth and meaning,
Make silent wishes all come true!

Fauve Fendt (13)
Dover Grammar School For Girls

THE CAT

A slender body with a curling tail
smooth black fur and bright green eyes
during the day he sits and sleeps
a harmless creature that's what you think,
but then at night that all changes
he searches for prey in the darkness
a mouse, rat, vole, he doesn't really mind
as long as it keeps up his healthy appetite,
bloodthirsty, a killer, harmful to others
that's it! he spots it, rustling in the grass
suddenly there is silence, but then he pounces
tearing it apart with teeth and claws.

A slender body with a curling tail
smooth black fur and bright green eyes
during the day he sits and sleeps
a harmless creature that's what you think!

Michelle Downey (11)
Dover Grammar School For Girls

ANIMAL KINGDOM

Where on Earth could one find
Trust without asking?
Love without competition?
Loyalty without doubt?

Where on Earth could one see
Beauty without vanity?
Peace with knowing war?
Man's hand yet still natural?

Where on Earth could one find
Friendship without bargaining?
Courage without armour?
Talent without bragging?

People who care,
I present to you,
The Animal Kingdom.

Nicola Pollard (12)
Dover Grammar School For Girls

GOING SHOPPING

As we approach the shopping centre;
I grab a trolley, then I enter.

Pushing slowly down one aisle;
I look around, give a cheeky smile.

I start to push a bit quicker;
Past the sweets, past the liquor.

My heartbeat racing;
As I'm quickly pacing.

Faster, faster past the fish;
Thinking of only one wish.

My wish not to bump into . . . *Mum!*
Oh no! I can see her come.

Rage, anger is what she feels;
Quickly I turn upon my heels.

That was the last day at the centre;
Now I won't ever enter.

Ria Sandilands (13)
Dover Grammar School For Girls

THE KITTEN TORMENTOR

They lay together,
With fear in their eyes,
Who will be first,
Dragged out miaowing and slashing their claws.

Children who saw this as fun and play,
Teasing the cats,
And running away.

But there's always one,
That hangs around,
Determined to hug and squeeze and play,
For squeezing a cat,
Who was not in the least bit pleased.

Through no fault of his own,
The cat had no choice,
A moment of panic,
And the slash of the claws . . .

So if you see a cat,
Just leave it alone,
Don't go teasing,
Or it will have no choice,
A quick clean cut,
And off you will run.

Carla Petch (12)
Dover Grammar School For Girls

DOLPHIN HAPPINESS

My dolphin is happy,
She jumps up and down.
She's getting excited,
And splashes around.
She likes to play and swim all day.

Swimming is great with this dolphin.
She is so elegant,
She is so glad,
She is so sad to leave me,
I am so sad to leave her.
I loved that dolphin,
But now she's swam away,
I hope I see her another day.

Samantha Taylor (12)
Dover Grammar School For Girls

SKULL

What used to be inside their heads?
What used to be in their beds?

They dreamt, they felt, they laughed, they cried.
Whatever did they feel inside?

What dreams they dreamt
Never did show.

What used to be
We will never know?

They dreamt, they laughed, they cried.
Whatever did they feel inside?

What used to be inside their heads?
Thinking and feeling but now they are dead.

They loved, they hated, they felt joy and pain,
Until the day that terror struck.

Megan Jones (13)
Dover Grammar School For Girls

AUTUMN

Autumn is here,
And so is the God.
The leaves are glistening,
From up above.
He walks around in his autumn suit.
As the leaves fall off the trees.

All the colours of the leaves,
Red, green, yellow and mellow,
Make a beautiful collage of colours.
Pears, apples, grapes galore,
Conkers and berries, what more?
As the leaves fall off the trees.

His fruity hat and his autumn bell,
He rings his bell to make a smell.
A rustic, English country smell,
As the leaves fall off the trees.

Katie Phillips (12)
Dover Grammar School For Girls

HALLOWE'EN

All was well one starry night,
Lamplights shining, the moon glowing bright.
Suddenly a bloodcurdling scream,
Echoed from by the motionless sea.

A madman was running along the pier,
Bloodstains all over his head.
Shouting for all to hear,
'Someone's murdered! Someone's dead!'

Silence hovered undisturbed,
Frozen solid, without a word.
Until another piercing cry,
Reflected from above in the towering sky.

Hubbub started, cries were heard,
The hovering silence was now stirred.
Someone was up there, doing a crime,
But all that moved was the ticking of time.

Sian Spicer (12)
Dover Grammar School For Girls

JANE EYRE

Jane Eyre
Alone in the red room
Jane Eyre
Beaten by your cousin
Jane Eyre
Hated by your aunt
Jane Eyre
Ten years old
Jane Eyre
Thin and scrawny
Jane Eyre
A new school, a ray of hope . . .
Jane Eyre
Rescued from the red room
Jane Eyre
Hope.

Carys Nia Williams (14)
Dover Grammar School For Girls

THE HIGH SCHOOL

The wind blowing chocolate wrappers around the dirty school,
The rain was a puddle of muck, and mud in the scruffy pool.
The road was a jam of cars and vans as the children poured out
                                                    of the gate,
And the children shouted 'It's Friday, Friday, Friday.'
The children cried 'It's Friday, and we're going home. It's great.'

With Reebok on his forehead, a ball of cotton at his chin,
A coat of the Ellesse sort, and the darkest skin.
His trainers came up to his ankles, and were tight on the thigh,
He rode a BMX Twinkle under the cloudy sky.

Over the pavement he raced quite fast into the old scrapyard.
Jumping over a bollard,
But the big, ugly policeman,
Bill, the policeman,
Banging his truncheon on the side of his leg.
Well what have you got to say for yourself?

Michelle Simmons (11)
Dover Grammar School For Girls

SPRING DRIFT

The air is just right,
The flowers have beauty,
The fields full of daisies,
And rich green grass.
A nice day for gardening
And children to play.
I hope forever, it will last, this day.
I hope forever it stays this way.

Yazmin Fisher (11)
Dover Grammar School For Girls

DOWN BY THE SEA

Down by the sea,
is a great place to be.
Playing in the sand,
is rather grand.

Splashing in the sea,
until it is time for tea.
Sitting in a deckchair,
breezes through my hair.

Riding on a donkey
up and down the quay,
all the little sailing boats.
I feel so
Free!

Rachel Attryde (11)
Dover Grammar School For Girls

SUKI

Suki the caring cat,
She's loveable, adorable.
She's not unlucky,
But she's black.
She's old and lazy
Like a sloth.
She's like a tiger throughout the day,
Hunting and catching her prey.
When she comes in,
She'll stretch and play,
And if she's tired she'll sleep all day.

Emma Cowens (12)
Dover Grammar School For Girls

MY BEST FRIEND

My best friend is two years old,
My best friend never feels cold,
My best friend never splits up with me,
My best friend is nearly three.

My best friend has a favourite rope toy,
My best friend is not a boy,
My best friend is brown and white,
My best friend is never in a fight.

My best friend is called Cassie,
My best friend also answers to Lassie,
My best friend chews on a pog,
My best friend is my *dog!*

Alex Topping (11)
Dover Grammar School For Girls

PREDATOR

Her padded pincushions lead into a corner
Where her stiff cotton thread whiskers
Pluck unsuspecting cobwebs with ease.
Her emerald eyes glow in the gloom
And with one fatal swipe
She reduces the spider to dust.
Behind the cabinet lies a graveyard of victims,
Each one craftily hidden.

Resuming her pose in front of the fire,
She purrs contentedly, feeling smug.
A cheeky smile bares her teeth,
Then very soon she drifts to sleep.

Amy Connolly (12)
Dover Grammar School For Girls

WAR II MEMORY

The rains of evil hatred
Fall down from the sky
As people hear the battle cry.
Children go away
Where war is nay.
Wives cry
As loved ones say goodbye.

Hitler's icy breath draws near
People run and hide in fear.
This is far worse
Than our first.
But we know
Winston Churchill.
Yes, Hitler fear this name,
For he shall lead us to victory.

Ahhhhhhhhhh.

Jennifer Byrne (11)
Dover Grammar School For Girls

MY SWEET TREAT

I'm gonna pop to the shop
To get a sweet to eat.
A brand new flavour,
For me to savour.
Red, yellow and green,
One I've never seen.
I've popped to the shop,
And got a sweet to eat.

Toniann Magrino-Daly (12)
Dover Grammar School For Girls

WHEN IT'S ALL OVER

As you turn on the TV,
You look at me,
And then turn to see the scenes of devastation in
New York City.
Nothing seems real,
As you stare at a defeated New York skyline.
Fire and smoke rule the heavens,
And you're not sure how to feel.
As the story unfolds,
Right before your tear-filled eyes,
Plumes of smoke fill the sun-kissed sky.
As it tries to sink in,
Your body tries to shut it out.
Something inside your head provides doubt.
Every part of your body aches with pain,
Hoping that by some small miracle,
Your lover missed their plane.

Samantha Horrobin (13)
Dover Grammar School For Girls

MY VERY BEST FRIEND

His coat is black and silky,
His nose is cold and wet,
The chappy in this poem,
He is my special pet.

I got him for my birthday,
He was just a furry ball,
He has now reached the age of five,
It seems no time at all.

He loves to go out for a walk,
He also likes to play,
His favourite game is hide-and-seek
That's how we end our day.

I love him more than ever,
Now this poem's going to end,
This little dog, his name is Sniff,
My very best friend.

Kellie Weaver (12)
Dover Grammar School For Girls

THE MERMAID

Her hair is golden piece of thread, swimming freely
in the salty water.
The salt glitters on her eyelids as she sits there on the rock
staring into the clear water.
The stunning mermaid swims in the bottomless blue ocean.
She swam and she swam until she came to a sandy beach.
She lay there all alone,
in the golden, scorching sand.
She pulls out a comb and combs her hair tenderly.
She holds the comb in her warm, soft tender hands,
and places it back.
Then with one gigantic leap she took one huge lungful of air and
jumped into the ocean and swam and swam until she reached where
she began.
She was the most beautiful young woman I had ever seen.

Dawn Glover (12)
Dover Grammar School For Girls

MY BROTHER'S A SOLDIER

My brother's a soldier,
I don't see him a lot.
My least favourite brother,
That he is not.

My brother's a soldier,
He drives a tank.
When he's at home,
I raid his bank.

My brother's a soldier,
He thinks he's the best.
He goes out there,
to beat the rest.

My brother's a soldier,
As sweet as could be.
But I think that could possibly,
Be only with me.

My brother's a soldier,
My family hero.
If he wasn't related,
I'd let him know.

Jodie Beer (11)
Dover Grammar School For Girls

LEARNING TO SWIM

As I stood there looking around,
The water came at me without a sound,
It swallowed me up,
Into its depth,
I started screaming,
And wouldn't rest.

Water poured into my mouth,
I wanted to shout,
But nothing came out,
Not even a sound,
I grabbed the side,
And gave a big sigh.

I hated water.

Laurence Biot (12)
Dover Grammar School For Girls

DEPENDENT, JANE EYRE

'You have no right to read our books,
No right to eat our food,
For you are a dependent, Jane Eyre . . .
Take her away to the red room.'

Taking my hair from my eyes,
I stared boldly around,
At that moment,
A light
On a wall.

This must be a vision,
A vision from another world,
My heart pounded inside me,
My body, hot.

Something seemed near me,
Too close,
Too close for comfort,
I rushed to the door,
Shook the lock,
No escape!

Amy Cole (13)
Dover Grammar School For Girls

COLOURS

Green is the grass
Fresh and bold
I hate the kind
That is brown and old.

Red is a ball
Shiny and round
Red is your heart
Ready to pound.

Yellow is the sun
Blaring and bright
It gives us heat
Not to mention the light.

Blue is the sea
Wild and rough
The sea is cold,
But that's just tough.

Pink is a love heart
It's there for love
A sign of peace
Is the white dove.

Kelly James (12)
Dover Grammar School For Girls

WITCH'S SPELL

Dancing around the cauldron's stew,
Add a rat's leg and a cup of dew,
Stir it around to make it froth,
Add a wasp's sting and half a moth,
Lizard's brain and frog's spit,
Skin of snake and baby's mitt.

Keep on boiling till night-time comes,
Add some blood and a witch's thumb,
Think of someone you wish to harm,
Inject the potion in their arm,
Stand around and watch them die,
Grind their bones to make a pie.

Alys Hewer (13)
Dover Grammar School For Girls

TWILIGHT ON THE BEACH

The waves are lapping the pebbly shore,
The water rises and splashes me,
Sitting lonely on the beach,
I see a wonderful shell in my reach.

I cry, I weep when I think of her,
Dying on this very beach,
It's not fair to be alive,
When I think she didn't survive.

As I see all the broken glass,
Stabbed in the chest below her breast,
Bleeding below the stars so bright,
I think of her every night.

In my dreams and my nightmares,
She appears in them all,
I think of her at home and during school,
All day and all night long.

Now it's time to leave this beach,
Think happy thoughts for a while,
Although I will be sad again,
I have to go, it's beginning to rain.

Nicola Reed (14)
Dover Grammar School For Girls

AUTUMN MORNINGS

The calm, delicate smell of autumnal atmosphere,
Floated peacefully,
Through the frozen breeze.
Gold sunlight shimmered,
As it hit the windows of the sleeping houses,
Which stood silently among the street.
A frost gradually grew from one end of the street,
To the other,
And as it grew, it laid a speckled sheet of dew on the
Grass as it passed.
Old, tatty leaves glided through the snoozing streets,
And rested on the path.
'Crunch, crunch!' Screamed the leaves,
As the postman strolled along the street,
Trampling on them all.
A dog and its owner returned from a long walk
In the fields nearby.
The walk was peaceful and pleasant.
The grass was covered in dew,
There was plenty of greenery and no one around.
A perfect place to go to think.
As early morning grew into late morning,
The sleeping birds awoke,
And sang a morning song to the street,
And the passers-by,
Like the milkman and the postman.
The morning was now wide awake,
With everyone out and about.
The speckled sheet of dew had now been lifted,
From the ground, by the sun.

Rachel McGarry (12)
Dover Grammar School For Girls

LOOK AT ME!

I hear people say
Your face is your fortune
Well that's okay,
But I see you look
Then turn away
Yes I'm different!

You stop and stare
Your face full of pity,
But you really don't care
I'm a person you know
You don't see what I wear
Yes I'm different!

But this is the face I was given
It's different from yours
And it's made me so driven
I thank my lucky stars
That I can be so forgiving
Yes I'm different!

Look deeper next time
Not at my face
You'll be surprised what you find
For I am not prejudiced,
But heartfelt and kind
Thank God that I'm different!

So remember next time you pass
This face shouldn't be judged
By beauty or by class
My heart is my fortune,
But what can you ask?

It's okay with me so, yes I am *different!*

Katie Clarke (12)
Dover Grammar School For Girls

WHY?

Why do we quarrel and fight?
When we can make the world right.

Why do the poor suffer?
When everyone has so much to offer.

Why do we go to war and destroy?
When we can live in peace and joy.

Why do we have to hurt others?
When we can live happily as brothers.

Do we have to
fight,
suffer,
destroy or
hurt others?
Why can't we make the world a better place,
and all live in harmony forever and ever?

Antara Banerjee (12)
Dover Grammar School For Girls

SOURCES OF LIGHT

The sun comes out in the day.
That's when you come out to play.
When the stars begin to peep.
That is when you go to sleep.
The moon joins the stars at night.
They give the world some light.

Suzanne Jones (13)
Dover Grammar School For Girls

SORRY!

'Hi, it's Miss Hadley, sorry I can't come in,
I have a bug.'
'Oh! Well don't do it again!'

'Hi, it's Miss Hadley, sorry I can't come in,
I broke my mum's *favourite* mug.'
'Oh! Well don't do it again!'

'Hi, it's Miss Hadley, sorry I can't come in,
I ran over a duck's beak.'
'Oh! Well don't do it again!'

'Hi it's Miss Hadley, I was wondering could I work another week?'
'Oh! Well don't . . . be late!'

Heather Goodsell (12)
Dover Grammar School For Girls

THE YOUNGEST

Do you know what it is like being the youngest?
Everyone expects you to do as well as your siblings.
No one listens to you or takes any notice.

Being the youngest, your older siblings
always expect more of you,
Your mum, always thinks you can do more,
You feel insecure, you are always being watched.

The youngest does have some high points.
People treat you as if you are seven years old,
and you feel happy.
Mum is kind and caring and always gives you cuddles
when you are feeling down.

Victoria Keeler (12)
Dover Grammar School For Girls

STORMY NIGHT

The wind whistled round the old oak tree
filling the air with its piercing noise.
The waxy surface of a leaf
was drummed by the waters of the Earth.
The soil is brown and swampy,
from the rain that washed it down.
The thunder roars,
and deafens creatures nearby.
The lightning flashes in the sky
filling the black with its blinding light.
This frightened night of flashes and crashes,
will all be over eventually.

Alex Phillips (12)
Dover Grammar School For Girls

HALLOWE'EN

H is for haunting, the night's really scary!
A is for awful, the spiders are hairy!
L is for light, little is found.
L is for lantern shining bright on the ground.
O is outfit, what one will you choose?
W is for witch with great pointed shoes.
E is for evil, the ghosts roam around.
E is for eerie, where are they found?
N is for now, 'cause now that you know,
   Hallowe'en is scary, wherever you go!

Chelsea Ramsay (12)
Dover Grammar School For Girls

ELMO

This newborn baby boy
Was a water baby.

Born on September 30th 2001
At 11:30 am.

He has a dad called Ian
And a mum called Grace.

He has a half-sister Rosie
And lots of cousins.

This newborn baby boy
Is my baby cousin Elmo.

Hannah Langley (12)
Dover Grammar School For Girls

THE RAIN

Pitter-patter, pitter-patter
Hailstones drizzle rain
Like someone tapping on my
Desk with their fingers
Pitter-patter, pitter-patter
Pitter-patter
Rain.

Megan Landman (11)
Dover Grammar School For Girls

HALLOWE'EN

Spooky! Spooky!
The witch's house,
Growl of dog,
Boil of pan.

Spooky! Spooky!
The witch's hall,
Creaky stairs,
Big brown doors.

Spooky! Spooky!
The witch's house,
Rusty beds,
Warm cup of tea.

Spooky! Spooky!
The witch's lounge,
Leather sofa,
Dusty sides.

Spooky! Spooky!
The witch's house,
Bats here,
Spiders there.

Spooky! Spooky!
The witch's bathroom,
Hot bathtub,
Dirty towel.

Spooky! Spooky!
The witch's house,
Down the corridor,
Through the door.

Spooky! Spooky!
The witch's kitchen,
Washing up,
Dirty floor.

Spooky! Spooky!
It's the witch's house!

Roxanne Skone (12)
Dover Grammar School For Girls

ANGER

The rage builds up inside,
It roars like thunder,
The fire in my stomach burns fiercely,
The flaming colours of red, orange and yellow zoom and flash
                                        past my eyes.

My skin feels hot,
My body becomes tense, my hands shake,
I hate it, there is so much anger inside me,
I feel like I'm going to explode, like a volcano ready to erupt.

The tiny hairs on the back of my neck stand on edge,
I want to throw things,
I need to relieve this rage; this stress inside me,
I feel so much hate.

I feel sick,
No one else understands; except me,
Sometimes I wish I could just disappear, be on my own, live my life,
I feel trapped; the anger is my partner.

I want to escape, be free from all this rage and pain, but,
Is there anyone who can help me; to tell me how?

Natalie Dowle (15)
Dover Grammar School For Girls

THIS IS MY PLACE

The horses are gentle giants
plodding round corners and up hill.
The mountainous shadows of the stable girls watch
over a herd of wooden stables.

I listen to the cornflake crunch of hay rustling
as horses munch, one eye on the green bucket
filled with chopped carrot.

The lush green field under my feet
is lined with small daisies. I suck on
a Polo that I can put my spongy tongue through.

This is my space . . .

Sometimes I want the ground to swallow me up
and take me to the fiery underworld.
Other times I feel like I'm on a wild stallion
strong and free.

Hollie Humphries (12)
Dover Grammar School For Girls

ICE CREAM

Ice cream tastes very good when it's hot,
It doesn't taste quite as good when it's not.
You can get it from the van,
You have to give your money to the ice cream man.

This is my favourite summer snack,
All year round you can buy it in a big or little pack.
This is the stuff that's very cold.
You have to have it in something to hold.

I think I've proved ice cream's cool,
Whether you're very big or very small.
You see children sitting eating it on walls,
We all agree ice cream rules!

Samantha Holness (12)
Dover Grammar School For Girls

ANNE FRANK

Concentration camp
Germans, evil and cruel
Dark, grey scary.

Left alone abandoned
Nobody there to love
Or care for me.

Wearing the yellow star identifying
Jews all over the world
Jews lying dead in 'graves'.

Possessions stolen from the family
Anne's house empty
Mother and sister murdered.

Anne Frank torn apart from loved ones
Crying out 'Why, Why?'

Hope has gone from Anne's heart
Anne's diary lies on the floor
Of the Frank family's secret annexe.

Anne's diary is read in years to come
All over the world young and old sit weeping
Reading the heart-rending story.

Francesca Parsons (13)
Dover Grammar School For Girls

CATS!

Cats' voices are sweet, silent and calm.
Cats' voices are loud, noisy and evil.
Cats' paws are hard and cold.
My cat is soft, warm and friendly.
My cat is scruffy, cold and evil.
My cat curls up in the morning,
My cat chases things at night.
The feline is nice and graceful,
The feline is fierce and quick,
The feline is asleep,
The feline is loudly awake.
At morning he is proudly grateful.
At night he is ferociously lithe.
At noon he is warm and cosy.
At midnight he is awake and a predator.

Stacey Salter (12)
Dover Grammar School For Girls

GOODBYE CRUEL WORLD

They hit me and kick,
They call me names,
I wait every day till 4 o'clock
To have it done again.

I cannot handle it anymore,
It hurts me too much.
They only have to say things,
They don't even touch!

I went home to my house,
I have had enough!
I went to the bathroom
There I saw the stuff.

I took it in my hand,
And held out my arm.
In the corner I curled,
And said to myself,
    Goodbye Cruel World.

Kelly Jarvis (13)
Dover Grammar School For Girls

HAM AND EGG

Ham and egg on my round plate,
Pass me a fork I just can't wait.
Splurt the ketchup on it too,
Bread and butter yes that'll do.
Dip it in my yolky egg,
But silly me it's on my leg.
Next I'll try to eat the chips,
Wow that's hot burning on my lips.
The ham is now all that's there,
For this fine meal I really care.
My tum is all full up now,
I feel like I just ate a cow.
I've got to rush see you soon,
I hope you like my little tune.
See you again perhaps next time,
You can sit and enjoy my rhyme.

Danielle Henry (13)
Dover Grammar School For Girls

FIREWORKS

Flashing like disco lights,
They sparkle, purples, greens and reds,
Twinkling like stars in the sky.

Rotating round and round again,
Spiralling, swirling, twisting,
They illuminate the sky.

Crackling, popping and banging,
Wriggling like worms,
They shoot into the sky.

Smoky clouds emerge,
from the golds and silvers,
that glow in the night sky.

Their arms,
Droop like branches on a willow tree.

Sonia Woolls (12)
Dover Grammar School For Girls

FRIENDS FOREVER

Friends forever always,
Until the very end,
Through bad times and good times,
Through going round the bend.

We make each other laugh,
We make each other cry,
We are both very truthful,
And never ever lie.

We are both bouncy and bubbly,
Kind, happy and mad,
We're wild, crazy maniacs
And will cheer you up if you're sad.

So if you're as good friends as we are
Such best friends then never
Give up such a great relationship,
And you'll be friends forever.

Rebecca McMahon (14)
Dover Grammar School For Girls

WHY?

Why do you live?
Why do you die?
Why do you laugh?
Why do you cry?

Why is there sun?
Why is there rain?
Why is there joy?
Why is there pain?

Why is there silence?
Why is there noise?
Why are there girls?
Why are there boys?

Why do these questions need answers at all?
Why can't we accept we can't know it all?

Kylie Scott (13)
Dover Grammar School For Girls

THE PREDATOR

The target is in position,
The predator is near,
Preparing for the lift-off,
The prey should have some fear.
The ears are pricked,
The tail is up,
The bristle coat is high,
An independent purring starts,
The prey begins to sigh,
It starts to creep up slowly,
The prey backs away,
Amber eyes pounce through the night,
And there the prey lay.

Amy Smallridge-Smith (12)
Dover Grammar School For Girls

WINTER

A chill fills the air,
All trees are left bare,
A cloud fills the sky,
Many plants die.

The frost spreads on the ground,
No animals to be found,
All in hibernation,
When food is a frustration.

As some people blink,
The sun starts to sink,
And it is clear,
Winter is here!

Dorinda Calvo (13)
Dover Grammar School For Girls

WHY?

Standing at the side of the rail,
Thinking about the past,
Was it my fault everything went wrong?
It's better if I am out of the way.

Here it comes.

I think about my childhood,
The good times,
Then the bad,
It makes me more determined.

I jump!

The train driver screams,
A crowd gathers to see the mess,
There's talk of why,
But they will never know
Why I had to get away.

Kiri Gordon (13)
Dover Grammar School For Girls

THE CAT DOWN THE LANE

The cat down the road, lives down the dark, damp lane,
Its wicked mind, a vicious claw
That stretches and is ready to swipe anything that comes too near,
Its dominant way, an ugly ear,
That was taken by a fight that needed no fear,
Its uneven fur-jagged teeth,
That are shown when eating its caught meat,
Its wild behaviour, its moody tail,
That moves to the beat without fail.

Katie Price (13)
Dover Grammar School For Girls

FELINE FRIENDS

I'm a photogenic puss,
With a perfect physique.
I hunt, I fight,
I claw and bite!
I'm so daring that I even hunt at night.

Suave and sophisticated,
I secretly stare,
At that stealthy black cat,
I gawpingly glare.

His fur so taut,
On his charcoal back,
So agile and sleek,
What a cool, crafty cat!

I use my padded, velvet paws,
To prolong no more;
I breathe and wait,
(The key is 'no haste')
Then take the moonlit-gilded floor.

I jump and jive and slide and glide,
All my way to him.

I smile and wink
And before I blink,
We're singing together
Under the starry night sky.

Imogen Vasey (12)
Dover Grammar School For Girls

CATS

Cats, peculiar creatures,
Prancing around with extraordinary features.

Let's take a look at the cats down the road.

First the one at number three,
Belongs to a little old lady (Mrs McKee)
Her cat, by the name of Hannah
Prowls around in a conspicuous manner.

Then there's Tom at number four.
He laps his milk then hints for more.
Then he lies basking in the sunshine,
And fondles his ear, making the most of his time.

Next, Mrs Brown's at number one
Chases around having fun.
When he creeps in, with his head down,
Mrs Brown gives him a frown.

While Mrs Smyth's at number nine,
Majestically sits on a cushion, oh so fine!
Pampered all day in a perfect state,
Miss Fluffykins, she thinks it's great.

Finally there's the cat that has no name.
He roams and wanders, what a shame!
He's thin and scabby and scrounges for scraps,
While all the others are in the warm, having a nap.

Kimberley Smith (12)
Dover Grammar School For Girls

SHARK!

Bathing in the cool blue sea,
I realise you're approaching me.
It's the telltale fin that gives you away,
That makes me want to frantically swim off,
But something persuades my trembling body to stop.

I try to be as still as I can,
Your beady, staring eyes piercing me with glaring rays.
As you get closer I wish I had swam,
Swam away out of danger.
I shut my eyes,
All I can do is wait silently, frozen,
Anticipating the dreaded moment.

Nothing happens,
I open my eyes,
Your great, magnificent size and power more apparent to me
as you circle me just inches away.
I pray that you will go away.

You continue to circle me,
Swiping your mighty tail from side to side.
Your gills move in and out like the tide,
I can't help but look at your dagger-like teeth,
Stained red.

Someone on the beach shouts *'Shark!'*
But I daren't even turn my head,
In case you think I'm alive, a juicy snack.
Finally you turn your back.
I wait until I can see the deadly fin no more,
Then I make a dash back to the shore,
Back to the shore where I'm safe from you.

Jessica Little (13)
Dover Grammar School For Girls

ASYLUM SEEKER

I look across the sea
There it is, my paradise
Or is it not what I'm expecting?
A warzone.

Here it comes, my transport.
Salvation
From my fate.

I hide, confused,
From the evil barrier
To a normal life.

I shrink myself, to fit under a car.

Nobody knows I'm there,
I think . . .
I move my foot, it makes a sound
Only a little one though.
Suddenly I hear
Footsteps
Slow
Loud
The hunters know I'm here,
That head lowers
I wait in terrible anticipation
Not knowing when they'll see me.

I look across the room
There it is, my nightmare.
People looking in at me, treating me like scum.
But maybe they've helped me see my paradise,
For what it really is.

Laura Patton (13)
Dover Grammar School For Girls

JANE EYRE

All alone and locked away
Red is what I see
Let me out, I think I may be mad
There's something there
Don't you see?
I shout and scream
But no one cares about me
They send me back
Back into there
As I filled up with red fear
It's Uncle Reed
He died, you see
In this room, in that bed
In the red room
But as I get more afraid
I collapse as I know there's something there
As alone and locked away
Red is what I see.

Louise Revell (14)
Dover Grammar School For Girls

LES FLEURS DE GUERRE

I walked through the field,
there was nobody there,
the poppies sighed together,
with the sadness in the air.

I heard a piercing cry,
as clear as it were day,
the cry of someone dying,
still brave when dead they lay.

The braveness of the soldiers,
felt strong in air around,
red poppies, not dead bodies,
were covering the ground.

Hannah Dixon (15)
Dover Grammar School For Girls

THINKING

When something happens, it makes you think
And you don't stop thinking until you get an answer,
If that answer is right,
You stop thinking and carry on;
But if that answer is wrong,
You start again.

Thinking, and thinking,
Things that went wrong,
Things that went right
And also the things that never happened . . .
But could have done.

It's those things that make you wonder,
The things that make you carry on thinking;
New thoughts keep entering your mind, until,
One day, you can't remember what you were thinking about.

You're back at the beginning,
With the same result as if you had the right answer to start with,
But all this time you've been thinking,
Thinking, and thinking,
Of what is wrong, and what is right.

So who is better off? The person with the right answer to begin with,
Or the person who stayed thinking?

Rachael Fletcher (15)
Dover Grammar School For Girls

WHY? WHO? WHAT? WHEN?

Every time I sit down and think why
Why do people kill and why do they die?
Every time I sit and think who
Who can kill yourself and take people with you?
Every time I sit down I think what
What is the point, the world hates them a lot?
Every time I sit down I think when
When will it end and lose this trend?

Every time I sit down and think why
Why do parents die and why do children cry?
Every time I sit down and think who
Who thinks they'll be heroes for doing what they do?
Every time I sit down and think what
What good are bombs because they hurt a lot?
Every time I sit down and think when
When will the killing stop and the world will become a friend?

Every time I sit down and think why
Why do people help and lose all the sighs?
Every time I sit down and think who
Who would all give up what they had to change the world from blue?
Every time I sit down and think what
What can I do to help these people a lot?
Every time I sit down and think when
When can I help the world which is condemned?

Lisa Howard (13)
Dover Grammar School For Girls

SCARED

Why was she hiding?
Why was she so unhappy?
She wanted to be alone,
The library seemed the best place to go.
Scared, she opened the door,
Silence met her face to face,
As she looked around
A stir of happiness lightened up the room.
Away from everyone,
Mrs Reed, Bessie, Abbot and especially evil John.
She picked up a book and began to read.
Past times gone and a feeling of freedom.
As she pulled the thick, red curtain around her
On the window sill,
A loud voice began to shout,
They found she was gone, and the sensation of freedom faded
As the voice came nearer.
Bang! The door flung open,
Where are you Jane?
Frightened she still hid.
But sadly she was seen,
Pulled out from the curtain,
Abused and tortured,
She screamed and screamed,
Until the scene closed in darkness.

Abigail Tyler (13)
Dover Grammar School For Girls

AMERICAN TRAGEDY

I return home from school like any other day,
the family all huddled around the telly.
The American Twin Towers blown to pieces,
thousands of innocent people dead.

The twisted tale seemed so fake and unreal,
the towers just fell like wobbling building blocks.
The upsetting pictures fixed on every channel on telly,
it was strange and confusing, nothing was right.

Depressed, upset and mourning the deaths,
all this because of one spiteful, selfish, dreadful man.
Why did he do it?
Why?

Hannah Kelly (13)
Dover Grammar School For Girls

FRIENDS!

To me a friend,
will always be there,
For me a friend,
will always care.

To me a friend,
will help you out.
To me a friend,
could scream and shout.

But remember a friend,
will always be there for you,
in the end.

Danielle Hammond (13)
Dover Grammar School For Girls

BEING BULLIED!

Being bullied is a horrible thing,
Pushed and pulled and punched and kicked.
Having your hair pulled out in chunks,
Fingers being slammed in doors!

Crying myself to sleep at night
I can't tell anyone.
I'm not a grass.
In any case it would just make it worse.

Suffer in silence, that's the way,
Bottle it up, keep it secret.
They will stop eventually, hopefully,
I can't take it any more, when will they stop?

They've got to stop before . . .
I . . .

Shannon King (13)
Dover Grammar School For Girls

THE RED ROOM

I shuddered as the great door slammed shut,
When they locked me in the red room.
So lonely on the cold, wooden floor,
My bruises throbbing.
The roof so tall, so dark,
Voices up there speaking to me.
My aunt will not believe me,
There's someone there,
There's someone there.

Victoria Bates (13)
Dover Grammar School For Girls

MEMORIES

I see myself lying, all tucked up in bed,
I can still smell the sweet stench of a tear that's been shed.
Is this reality or is this a dream?
I find myself thinking of the times that have been.
The times of the pain and the times of the sorrow.
What could have happened in the days of tomorrow?
Would I be happy or would I be sad?
I look back and think of the days that I've had.
The days of the suffering and the days of the pain,
The days of the agony and the days of the shame.
But the times of the happiness, the fun that we shared,
The time and the effort of someone who cared.
The love and affection that you'd always shown,
Those long conversations we'd have on the phone.
You made me feel normal, you made it all clear,
You helped me through the bad times and wiped clean my tears.
I'll always remember how you helped me to live,
The shoulder to cry on that you'd always give.
So please don't be sad and please don't you cry,
As I leave you alone and I say my goodbye.

Louise Campbell (16)
Dover Grammar School For Girls

RIVERBANK DITTY

All along the riverbank
Badgers are asleep,
Toads are abustling,
And weasels creep.

The fish are swimming
The hedgehogs all curl up,
Stoats are agabbling
And mole is fed up.

The ducks are apecking
At the rushes tall.
One's eating bread
And one's in Toad Hall.

The foxes howl
And give a loud call
To the vixens
Who are sniffing around Toad Hall.

Sarah Trafford (14)
Dover Grammar School For Girls

TO BE A BIRD

I long to be way up there, in the sky, in the air,
Feeling the wind in my hair.

If I was a bird up in the clouds, looking down on crowds.
Laughing at their worries.

I wouldn't have any worries, any problems would brush away,
They would flit off like pieces of paper.

As you fly towards the sunset, your heart feels content,
The purple reflects onto your pupils.

Or flying over the warm blue blanket, the boats sliding,
Sliding on the blanket like skaters on ice.

If only I could hear things from a high flyer's point.
It would probably be drowned out by tranquillity.

Oh what it would be to be a bird,
It would fill my heart with happiness.

Ellie Cox (13)
Dover Grammar School For Girls

It Cascades

Long and thick it runs to Earth,
Creating nature's pattern as it goes,
Befriending it, the two great powers,
Enraged at the outcast they've become.

Thick and long it cascades forever downwards,
Forgetting the form it once was told.
Now regretful and laughing to itself,
Tumbling up as it meets its beginning's end.

Long, thick streams,
As in a dream.
Falling beams,
Its lusting team.

Never stop, ever stop, forever stop,
Twisting the destined path it never wanted to follow.
Again it laughs and clenches fists,
To remind all who it is.

Rosie Cracknell (15)
Dover Grammar School For Girls

The Skull

A dead yellow head
Lying in a bed
Eye sockets as black as night
The funeral service so bright.

His spirit still lives on but he never will
Flowers scattered around so still
This deserted place
And his hard hollow face.

There he is lying
Hair long and dying
Deaf and blind
He has lost his mind.

There he lies
No one cries
Lone and gone
He has stopped his song.

Megan Georgiou (12)
Dover Grammar School For Girls

BLURRED

Every person was in silence,
but I could feel violence.
The day would be cold,
or so I was told.
The furnace fired,
so I retired.
The fire blazed,
but I wasn't fazed.
Voices started to get deep
and I fell asleep.
In the action dream I was brave,
but I ended up in a grave.
I felt the way anyone would feel,
if you had a dream that was so real.
From my sleep I was stirred,
but my memory and vision were blurred.

Lucy Perrow (14)
Dover Grammar School For Girls

PEAS

'Mum, Mum,' I said, 'I don't like peas,
I get a rash, spots and deafness
And I can't pronounce my Ts.'

'Mum, Mum,' I said, 'I don't like peas,
They make my eyeballs go bright green
And they taste of gone-off cheese.'

'Mum, Mum,' I said, 'I don't like peas,
They're not really from Tesco's,
But from alien trees.'

'Mum, Mum,' I said, 'I don't like peas,
Don't make me eat these mushy balls,
I'm begging you Mum, please!'

Natalie Georgiou (15)
Dover Grammar School For Girls

I THINK OF YOU OFTEN

Sometimes when I sit alone,
Amongst the green, grassy slopes
That I call my home,
I wonder and whisper your name.

Softly you would cradle me
In your warm, welcoming embrace,
Gently coaxing and encouraging,
A peaceful, sleepy silence.

Sometimes when I sit alone,
Glistening tears trickle down my cheeks,
I see your shimmering silver hair
And wish you were near.

Sophie Wolfenden (15)
Dover Grammar School For Girls

LOSS OF A LOVED ONE
(In loving memory of our golden boy - Joseph Daniel Sales)

The pain inside my heart still hurts, the tears
hiding in my eyes still fall.
With every stir a memory, a happiness now so sad,
a waking call.
My life is not now as it used to be,
everything I encounter comes back to you and me.
The stars in the sky twinkling bright, the morning rain
showering through the light.
Sad songs of sorrow on the radio, my sadness for your
departure does show.
I can see you now, your angelic face, the smell of hair gel,
perfectly in place.
The whisper of the morning sun fills me with sadness,
I'm sure you see, that the sun has no happiness now,
that you're no longer here with me.
That striking smile and those piercing eyes, see deep
within my soul.
Not only do you mean the world to me, but you're
my everything, my happiness, my all.
Your words so gentle, your embrace so warm.
The day you were taken and walked on by, my world
became a storm.
We all miss you more than words can say, we know
that you're with us every hour of every day.
We just find it hard because you were the one, looked
upon and loved by everyone.
Goodbye for now, the lights are beginning to dim,
if ever I knew a gentleman, you were him.

Always in our thoughts, loved and remembered.

Anna-Nadia Tweed (16)
Dover Grammar School For Girls

NO MURDERER COULD BE SICKER
THAN THE EVIL SINNER - JACK THE RIPPER!

He was so unnoticed,
A man so unseen,
But this helped to plot
His murderous scheme

Eddowes, Chapman and Kelly,
Tall, young and fair,
Didn't know of their fates
And remained unaware!

Buried in the shadows,
He took out his knife,
Cut open her throat -
Which took Chapman's life.

He killed once more,
She died in pain,
This victim was second -
Eddowes was slain.

Kelly was third,
To Dorset Street she'd go,
But met by death -
He was now London's foe.

The police were frantic,
They called Scotland Yard,
No one knew his identity,
The investigation was too hard.

Who he was, we don't know,
He was just too clever.
Maybe someday we'll find out -
Or maybe we won't - ever!

Jade Everett (13)
Dover Grammar School For Girls

JANE EYRE

Jane Eyre,
Orphan,
Unloved, poor and ill-treated.
John Reed's
Victim,
Bullied, hit and hurt.
Daring to hit back,
Banished
To the red room,
Cold, dark and ghostly.
Hours passed.
A ghostly light
Travelled across the wall.
Was this the ghost of Uncle Reed?
Terrified Jane collapsed.

Later,
Safe in her nursery bed,
Jane expressed a wish, to go to school,
A better prospect than Gateshead.

Months passed with no news.
Then one morning,
Mr Brocklehurst arrived.
Jane was to go to Lowood School.
There to be made
Useful.
To be kept
Humble.
Vacations to be spent at Lowood.
Could this be worse
Than Gateshead?

Catherine Renault (13)
Dover Grammar School For Girls

JANE EYRE

Bullied and tormented by your cousin John Reed
His mother just looks past you
Believing only her son
Bruises and pains ignored as she shouts
'Send her to the red room!'
Trapped in this room hour after hour
Terrified of ghostly apparitions
Kicking, screaming, weeping
Exhaustion makes you ill
Then hope! Your friend
Your saviour? Mr Lloyd
Hope is in the distance
For you are off to school.

Kathryn Williams (13)
Dover Grammar School For Girls

IN THE EYES OF JANE EYRE

Here I stand alone again,
Staring at bleak red walls.
Punished for defending myself at Gateshead Hall.

Breathing his last in this dismal place,
If only he was alive to save me from these taunts.
'Unjust! Unjust!' I screamed.

Bessie held my hand and sympathised,
Whilst Mrs Reed displeases with my cries.
Another hour until I was freed.

Rebecca Grew (13)
Dover Grammar School For Girls

THE RED ROOM

I'm sitting up here all alone
Looking into space
I look again, I take a breath
I'm shocked, I see a face

I bellow and scream
And shout for help
A maid comes running by
I can't believe that she could think
My story is a lie

The mistress comes
She shouts at me
I slip into a daze
And dream of when I sing and shout
Oh those were happy days.

Emma Hodge (13)
Dover Grammar School For Girls

JANE EYRE

'You're always bad,' says Mrs Reed.
But I don't know what I've done
I don't know how to do things right
I always seem to do them wrong
I try to do things right, but can't
They always say I've done them wrong
All in all I do not think it's fair
That everything I do is wrong.

Helen Nolan (13)
Dover Grammar School For Girls

JANE EYRE

I feel sorry for her
The girl they call Jane Eyre
Her parents died when she was young
All she needed was a little care
She was sent to live with her uncle
But then he died too
She was stuck with nasty Mrs Reed
What was a girl to do?
And the story I heard
When she started to scream
She had a vision
Or some say it was a dream
Was it true? Maybe not
Did she see a ghost?
Was it a mirage?
Maybe it was the bedpost
For a while she was ill
All of a few days
When Abbot and Bessie saw her ill
They were all amazed
I feel sorry for her
The girl they call Jane Eyre
Her parents died when she was young
All she needed was a little care.

Hollie Lee (13)
Dover Grammar School For Girls

ME!

He hit me! I will never forget the moment when he hit me,
A large axe striking my head.
I reeled like an overbalanced chair.
A blinding flash before my eyes.
A trickle running warm over my flesh.

She lectured me! I will never forget the lecture she gave me.
'I am a deceitful child with a sinful heart
I am stony and cold and deserve nothing
More than Satan to warm my blackened soul!'

They locked me up! I'll never forget when they locked me up.
I have arrived in my makeshift hell.
Red furniture, red walls . . .
Red searing the backs of my eyes.
I see a light, my saviour.
Fear takes hold.
It's coming over.
Red to black.
Gone!
I wake up and see a doorway of hope.
Mr Lloyd vanishes like all my hopes.

They hate me! I will never forget how they hated me.
Let them never forget.
I will hate them till the day I die.
Let them never forget me.
Jane Eyre!

Hannah Taylor (14)
Dover Grammar School For Girls

JANE EYRE

Here I am in the red room,
The door slams, I'm left alone.
At the end of the bed is a table covered
With a crimson cloth,
I dared not cough.
I have visions of ghosts,
I see lights as if ghosts are there.
I shock the lock on the door,
I hear the steps on the outer passage
Coming along,
Bessie and Abbot, along they come,
I hate this red room,
Let me out!
Mrs Reed locked me back in,
Here I am in the red room, alone or not?

Maria Duran (14)
Dover Grammar School For Girls

MAKE-BELIEVE

I make-believe that the flowers
grow big and tall and grand.
I make-believe that the butterflies
fly straight into my hand.
I make-believe the wind blows
me far, far away.
I make-believe all sorts of things
and that is how I play.

Kimberley Turner (12)
Dover Grammar School For Girls

ALONE

All alone in the Red room.
She sits, waits, glares.
All alone in the Red room,
For someone to notice she's there.

Mr Reed had died in that room,
She knew that was true,
Mr Reed had died in that room,
She had seen his ghost there too.

She screamed and screamed and screamed once more,
But no one listened, no one cared,
She screamed and screamed and screamed once more,
Until there was five minutes to be spared.

Elizabeth Morton Baged (13)
Dover Grammar School For Girls

JANE EYRE

I'm really lonely
I hate this room!
I'm feeling lonely
I hate this room!
My head is spinning
I hate this room!
I'm feeling faint
I hate this room!
I just screamed
I hate this room!
I hear people coming
I hate this room!

Helen Stubbs (13)
Dover Grammar School For Girls

Jane Eyre 'In That Ghostly Room'

Sitting, staring into the darkness of the room,
Not knowing what happened in that ghostly room.
Out on the lawn there was a figure,
A ghostly figure out on the lawn.
The next thing I knew,
The window's thrown open,
The shutters thrown up,
A howling gale released into the red room.
Sitting, screaming,
A figure appeared,
I felt myself falling deeper and deeper.
I awake to the blood-red glow
Of the nursery fire.
A kind and gentle hand,
Laid on my head,
A few kind words
From a kind and caring heart.
My dear friend Bessie,
My foe Abbot,
My evil minder Mrs Reed,
Who locked me up,
Called me a liar and a treacherous snake
And vanished me into the depths of that ghostly room.

Gina Winthrop (13)
Dover Grammar School For Girls

SABRE

Can you lie and fill the floor space?
Can you drink out of the loo?
Do you chew shoes and leave the lace?
And do you need others to clear up your poo?

Are you always left in the hall
When everyone goes out?
Do you make your bed look small
When really it is not?

I'm furry and sweet,
I get found in the pound,
I have blooming big feet,
That's right, *I'm a greyhound.*

Leah Baker (12)
Dover Grammar School For Girls

THE SNAKE

It meanders like a river,
As silent as an assassin,
Its teeth as sharp as an owl's beak.

It sees its prey . . . a rat,
And silently slithers,
It opens its mouth and the rat is gone.

It's as fast as a cheetah,
It's small,
But one day it will be large.

Alan Dewsnap (14)
Hartsdown Technology College

LIFE

Life is just like a flower,
As you go through many
Different changes,
Just like a flower grows
New petals and buds,
Flowers lose strength
Like we lost battles.

As a flower grows, it is nourished,
As we are nourished
By family and friends.
As it falls down,
Someone picks it up.
When we fall down,
We carry on being ourselves.

As the flower begins to fade,
So we fade too.
People around us become quite sad,
Like the creatures in plants,
We turn to a fresh start in a different world.

Alisha Dixon (13)
Hartsdown Technology College

BULLYING IS . . .

Like a venomous snake that won't let go.
Like a crocodile's mouth - dangerous.
Like a boa constrictor's grip.
Like a sabre-toothed tiger bite.
Like a pike that won't let go of a smaller fish.
Like a strong person who takes advantage of a weaker person.

James Heathorn (13)
Hartsdown Technology College

BULLYING IS . . .

Like an unfathomable maze - it's never-ending.
Like a past you can't forget - it plays on your mind.
Like a venomous snake that won't let go.
Like an over-hanging wall you can't climb without a rope.
Like a skin you can't shred.
Like a shadow you can't escape.
Like handcuffs without a key.

Marc Wood (13)
Hartsdown Technology College

BULLYING IS LIKE . . .

A deep hole that you can't get out of.
Going round and not finding the right way out.
A snake wrapping tightly around you.
Hearing a tap dripping continuously in a silent room.
A bad dream that is still in your mind when you wake up.
Being pushed into a corner which you can't escape from.
Being suffocated with a plastic bag.

Andrew Parker (13)
Hartsdown Technology College

BULLYING IS . . .

Like an unfathomable maze - never-ending.
Like a hole of dead souls.
Like being lost at sea for days, thinking will I be rescued?
Like never being able to wake from a nightmare.
Like being in gloom forever.
Like being trapped in a black hole in total darkness.

Benjy Smith (13)
Hartsdown Technology College

BULLYING POEM

Bullying is . . .
Like an unfathomable maze, it's never-ending.
Like a deep black hole which you can't escape from.
Like a snake around your, really tight.
Like a heavy weight that you cannot break free from.
Like a horror movie that never ends.
Like something that you can't get rid of.

Daniel Akhurst (13)
Hartsdown Technology College

BULLYING IS . . .

Like someone is thumping you to the beat of your heart,
like weights on your body dragging down,
like the pain of a wasp that keeps stinging you,
like the whips of a belt that's lashing you,
like the gates of a prison cell not letting you out,
like a punchbag that keeps getting punched,
like a sound in you year that won't go away.

Andrew Bennette (14)
Hartsdown Technology College

BULLYING

Like a crown of evil
Like a hole of fire
Like a square of black flames
Like a red raw rage
Like a desperate distraction
Like a bitter taste of fear
Like a message that will never go.

Kimberley Elmes (13)
Hartsdown Technology College

A STORY OF WAR TOLD BY A MAN OF PEACE

I'm only twenty years old
I've been given a gun to hold
I'm sitting in a trench in Normandy
About to fight the enemy.
The bullets are flying all around,
But the sergeant said to stand our ground.
My body is trembling with fear,
A German shell has dropped quite near.
We all stand full of fear,
Knowing the enemy is here.
As I look all around,
I see dead bodies on the ground,
A shout goes out, we must attack,
We must go forward and never look back.
We are moving forward all the time,
We are across the enemy line,
As we go round one more bend,
We pray this war will come to an end.

Luke Adams (13)
Hartsdown Technology College

BULLYING IS . . .

Like an unfathomable maze, it's never-ending.
Like a day that will never end, it torments you forever.
Like a scar you can never get rid of.
Like a nightmare you never wake up from.
Like an experience you will never forget.
Like a boot that will never stop kicking you.
Like a never-ending headache, it just goes on and on.

Kerry Mann-Taylor (13)
Hartsdown Technology College

BULLY

I get on my tie, I'm dreading school,
I get called names like pig, or fool,
They shove me over and call me thick,
It's really not fair that they take the mick.
Straight away I walk through the gates,
No one to wait for, I have no mates,
I'm scared and I'm petrified,
Tears fill my eyes, I could have cried.
They give me a kick and then a punch
And then run away with my big and lunch!
I knew that I would never be free,
They said, 'Don't tell' or they'd kill me!
Well I had to tell someone,
But they'd beat me up, that won't be fun.
I knew I had to, I built up courage,
My knees were wobbly like sloppy porridge.
'Please Miss, I'm gonna die.'
'I'm sure you won't, now, do not cry.'
Another day tomorrow,
Can I face it?

Ysabelle Bradshaw (11)
Hartsdown Technology College

BULLYING IS . . .

like a crown of evil,
like a stab in the back,
like a circle of fire,
like a bull seeing rd,
like a hole of death,
like a threat of life.

Sean Robinson (13)
Hartsdown Technology College

WAR

War: what a horrible thing!

Some call it a game,
Some call it a tournament.

What do I think of war?

It is something the world could do without,
Skies slashed,
Torn heavens reigning blood,
The bitter taste of defeat in killers' mouths,
War sounds the fatal bell of a thousand cries.

There is no such thing as a winner in war,
Only hearts are cleaved in two.

Tim McArthur (14)
Hartsdown Technology College

WHIZZIPIG

The whizzipig is a fast little critter,
He has big wings that do glitter.
As it travels at speeds of light and sound.
But the whizzipig causes quite a titter,
For he can be heard, but not found.

Man can try to find him,
But they will only fail,
For few men know
That this pink, shiny glow
Is not the whizzipig, for the whizzipig is only a fable.

Christopher Marsh (13)
Hartsdown Technology College

ALONE AT NIGHT

The sun is setting in the sky
It's time for it to say goodbye

Little children asleep at night
As their mothers switch off the light

All that is in sight is a cardboard box
Inside is a stray old fox

Up in the sky are beautiful stars
That glisten all around the planet Mars

In the street, the lamps are bright
Not a single person is around at night

And when the sun starts to peep
The little children awake from their sleep.

Carrie Couldridge (14)
Hartsdown Technology College

WAR THAT NEVER GETS ANYWHERE

War is stupid because it doesn't get anywhere.
War just kills more men every day.
There are never any winners just losers.
It doesn't solve anything.

But yet men go to war because they're told it's fun,
But when they get into war they soon wish they'd never come.
All that happens is men die and others watch them die.

Sarah Burnett (14)
Hartsdown Technology College

MY ANIMAL

This animal wakes up quite late,
Sometimes it sleeps for half the day.
It has thin, brown eyes
And short brown hair.

It doesn't live in the trees
Or in the water,
It lives on land
Like you and me.

It eats plants and meat
And enjoys the heat,
But enjoys the cold as well.

This animal may be related
To me and maybe you.
This animal is over five feet tall,
This animal is my sister!

She's scary when she wakes up,
I try and stay out of her way.
She goes out nearly every day,
But sometimes stays at home.

She's also nice,
It's hard to believe,
But she helps me with my homework,
She also listens when I speak
And buys me shoes and clothes.
Sometimes she may be horrible,
But after all, she is my sister!

Kirsty Ramshead (13)
Hartsdown Technology College

I Am A Leaf

I am a little leaf
Swaying in the tree,
All of my friends have gone on holiday, I think
And they have all just left me.
Now I am alone
And need a safe place to go,
My home is swaying really hard,
Help, help me, oh no!

Now I am really hurt and
I want my mum and dad,
My mum can solve anything, even when I am sad.
Now I know where my friends have gone,
They have fallen on the lawn,
Ouch! Someone has just trod on me
And now I am all torn.

Shane O'Connor (13)
Hartsdown Technology College

War Poem

Bombs, bullets, death and blood
Bodies lying in the mud
Soaring planes just like birds
Their bombs are coming
They never turn.

Injured men crying just like kids
Crying for help
They never cease
They sit there all night and day
Unable to move, they rot away

Doctors and nurses viewed as kings and queens
They are lifesavers drifting through the breeze
Manage to reach the lucky few
You lie there hoping they're coming for you

Too much death and too much blood
Can it stop? Why did it start?

Douglas Sinclair (14)
Hartsdown Technology College

AUTUMN

Leaves glitter on the trees
As children go home with dirty knees.
The moon is shining brightly
With a glowing light.

The wind is blowing,
More leaves are going
Orange, red and brown,
In the parks, suburbs and towns.

As the first frost comes down
The leaves turn brown.
Darker and darker the nights will get,
Colder and colder we will get.

Four o'clock it gets dark,
The restless dogs begin to bark.
Five o'clock, it looks like night,
Lamplights leer from an eerie height.

Leaves glitter on the trees,
While children go home with dirty knees.
The moon is shining brightly
With a glowing light.

Natasha Collins (13)
Hartsdown Technology College

AUTUMN TO WINTER CHANGES

Changes are starting,
Changes are happening.
Leaves on trees are turning,
Orange, yellow and brown.

As the wind blows
The leaves twirl and whirl,
Twist and turn,
Go crashing to the ground
Without a sound.

Changes are starting,
Changes are happening,
It's too late to stop it now,
The trees have all gone bare.
Snowflakes are falling all around me,
Christmas is here.

In every house you can hear
The ripping of wrapping paper
And the screaming of young children,
Excited by their presents.

Changes have happened,
Changes have finished,
For now at least.

Abby Scarr (13)
Hartsdown Technology College

MY FIRST WEEK OF HIGH SCHOOL

In my first week of high school
I made so many friends
And had so many lessons,
I don't know where it ends!

On my third day of high school
The windows started to leak
And basically that's what happened
During my first week.

Caroline Crouch (12)
Hartsdown Technology College

ANGELS

I know it's sad
And I know it's not funny,
But don't feel sorry
When someone you know
Goes to Heaven
If you cry it makes you feel better,
But sometimes it doesn't
It makes you scream and go wild
You may not know, but whoever
You miss who has gone away
Watches you day and night
They're like your own personal angel
Guarding you throughout the day and night
You never know, they might
Come and visit when you're
Feeling sad or maybe
Even happy
I know how you feel because
It's happened to me a lot of times
I've even thought of going up there
With them, but as we all know
We all go to Heaven sooner or later
And they will be waiting for you
To join them.

Vicky Mann (13)
Hartsdown Technology College

MY BROTHER

Mum's coming home,
Mum's coming home,
She's coming home today.

Mum's bringing a very special present.
I've waited for so very long
And things won't be the same.

I can't wait to hold it in my arms.
She's walking up the path now,
Like a postman with his parcels.

I open the door to welcome in
Family member number four.

Matthew Shurmer (13)
Hartsdown Technology College

NIGHT-TIMES

Night-times, night-times
Night-times are dark
Night-times are scary
Night-times are filled with ambition and dreams.

The big and small, dark
Creepy shadows hiding in
The alleyway.

Then daylight approaches
And the big and small, creepy
Shadows turn into wild cats and dogs.

Clare Vincer (13)
Hartsdown Technology College

HARTSDOWN COLLEGE

H artsdown is my new school
A fraid of being bullied or getting lost
R un to my form, can't be late
T ime for break
S ee my friends, go and play
D on't know what to do
O h time to go, the pips have gone
W ait for the teacher to call my name
N ext lesson time to go.

C lose my pencil case, open my book, time for work
O ops spelt that wrong, cross it out and start again
L isten to the teacher while she explains homework
L ook at the clock, time to go
E at my lunch with my friends
G o to the fields and look around
E veryone shoves to get to our next lesson.

Hayley Kelly (11)
Hartsdown Technology College

AUTUMN!

A ll the leaves fall from the trees.
U nder the brown, crisp leaves you can find acorns and fir cones.
T rees shake in the blustery wind.
U nderneath leaves or on the corners of roads, children
rummage for conkers.
M erry children collect conkers from the ground.
N ow autumn has come to stay for a season before winter arrives.

Rebecca Spencer (13)
Hartsdown Technology College

TERROR IN AMERICA: A TRIBUTE

How come one can hijack a plane?
Nothing to lose and nothing to gain,
Killing the humane,
No more chance of surviving in a world others are alive in,
As innocent people are dying, millions of people are crying.

But a man with a sad message loves being aggressive,
Can cause so much pain,
And love is wiped out by a plane.
Leaving a country saddened in shame,
Knowing just who to blame.

A man who hijacks a plane
Is dumb and should be ashamed,
A coward, a freak,
Can't even speak,
Can't read words,
It's absurd.

So, take a glance,
And give peace a chance,
And you will see it there,
A world that cares.

Lawrence Hollett (13)
Hartsdown Technology College

NIGHTFALL

As the summer's day ends and darkness falls
You can hear the sweet sounds of robins' calls

Calling for their mum to return to their nest
To comfort them and love them like mums do best

I hate the dark, it frightens me sick
Like a tall, dark shadow as thin as a stick

The streets are quiet, not a sound
Only the milkman doing his round.

Clare Stevens (13)
Hartsdown Technology College

THE SCHOOL BOY

I love to wake on a winter's day
When the hot, open fire is warming me,
I can go to the fridge to get some marshmallows to cook on
the open fire.

I cook them until they are black and brown,
Oh what a great feeling,
To eat hot marshmallows.

But to go to school on a winter's day,
Is freezing my hands and feet,
It makes me feel like a human freezer.
The teachers act as if they don't care about the cold,
And the Year 7s spend the day laughing and playing,
Looking like they're not bothered about the cold.

When I'm there I want to be warm and have cocoa
And worry if the warm fire will still be lit.

I can't do my work with cold hands,
I just don't want to be at school in the cold.
How can we be expected to do work with cold hands
Or keep our minds on mind?
Why must we go to school on a winter's day?

Simon White (14)
Hartsdown Technology College

My Version Of William Blake's 'The School Boy'

I love to wake up on a winter's day,
When the snowman comes out to play.
I can go to my nan's and play
And stay forever and a day.
Oh what joy I have today!

But to go to school on a winter's day,
Oh! It takes all great enjoyment away.
The teachers act so cruel and mean
And the year 7s spend their day playing,
But look - there is a magpie which brings sorrow today.

When I'm there I feel great sorrow in my heart
And worry about what I'm missing.
I can't enjoy a winter's day,
I can't go out with the snowman and play.
I just don't want to have this sorrow in my heart.

How can we be expected to have enjoyment
Or play all day?
Why must I have this sorrow all day?
And why can't we be joyful and happy?
It makes me all so glum!

Victoria Britton (14)
Hartsdown Technology College

Stars

S tars shining brightly in the night sky
T winkling in the beautiful dark sky
A s night settles in
R ocking side to side, the stars shine brightly
S hooting stars light up the dark, cloudy night.

Ian Swift (13)
Hartsdown Technology College

WAR

War is stupid, never gets anywhere,
In war there are no winners or losers.
People die, others don't,
Young boys think war is great, fantastic,
A game, they have not seen what it is like.
Old men don't because they've experienced the horror of war.
War is like a game of chess that never ends and no one wins.
How would you feel if you had to leave your country?
Some people your age do.
All because of war.
War is a hand that grips people's lives.
If you had to leave all your belongings behind,
Your friends, family and home,
How would you feel?
Other people do.
Now through this you might be able to see how horrific war is.
So perhaps in your short lifetime you can do all you can do
To try to stop all of this from happening.

Hannah Skull (14)
Hartsdown Technology College

SOUND AND SIGHTS

The lovely colours of the flowers in the spring
The beautiful shape of a robin's wing
The richness of the grass so green
And like the flow of a water stream
A petal of a rose falling slowly to the ground
And the little baby squirrels running around and around
The sun rising up behind a tall oak tree
These are some sounds and sights that are precious to me.

Jodie Bing (13)
Hartsdown Technology College

SCHOOL

H artsdown is a very good school
A rt is my favourite lesson
R ed is the colour of a rose
T op marks is my favourite
S chool is just the best
D irty floors makes the school all dirty
O utdoors is for playing
W inning races is good
N asty boys are bullies

C ool teachers
O range drinks
L azy people not doing lessons
L oads of nice teachers
E lectrical stuff is fun to use
G ood teachers help us learn
E verywhere laughing people.

Scott Young (11)
Hartsdown Technology College

AUTUMN!

The leaves fall to the ground,
Where acorns cannot be found.
When it gets dark, no one is in the park.
The sun comes out and people are about.
The rain starts to fall, no one can play ball.
Autumn is a wonderful thing,
It gives you a brilliant feeling.

Lauren Edwards (13)
Hartsdown Technology College

ENGLISH AND RE

E   veryone must like the English teacher
N   ever any lack of behaviour
G   o run it's English next
L   ovely paragraphs are what we're learning about
I   t is nice to be safe in lesson
S   ometimes people mess about
H   elp! Help! I want to go to English.

R   unning to RE
E   very lesson I wish I was with my RE teacher
L   earning about other religions
I   t's fun
G   od is everywhere
I   n everything
O   beying religious rules
U   sually we get merits at the start
S   ometimes it goes quick, sometimes it goes slow.

Charity Styles (12)
Hartsdown Technology College

NIGHT-TIME

While certain animals sleep at night,
The fox and the owls come out to fight
And while the stars are shining bright,
The moth flaps its wings with all its might.
The reflections in the water of blue are so clear
To see as you and me.
The moon shines forth at a great height
And people watch and think what a wondrous sight.

Samantha Howard (14)
Hartsdown Technology College

WALKING TO SCHOOL

I am walking to school up the alley
I try to walk further but all I hear
Is children's happy laughter
I want to join in but I have to go to school
Unlucky me, I am not cool
My friends don't even like me
Which I think is so unfair,
But all they keep on doing is pretending I'm not there
My family ignores me and I get upset
Whenever they want me, I say 'No, not yet'
I don't like being bullied
I hate not being you.

Carly Winter (11)
Hartsdown Technology College

WAR!

The screams of hell
Like a giant bell
People dying here and there
Guns being shot everywhere
The blood in the air
And buildings explode in the air
Lives cut short
People dying in their fort
The bodies of the dead
People shot in the head
Then it is silent
The people are gone.

Ben Newman (13)
Hartsdown Technology College

SCHOOL

I   n the morning I get dressed

L   earning is hard, but a bit fun
I   like school, but it is boring
K   icking and punching is a school rule
E   ducation hurts my brain

S   ometimes I need fun to keep me sane
C   an't go on I'm getting tired
H   omework is hard and confusing
O   ften I work hard
O   ut of school I play with friends
L   ast week before half term.

Kieran Cox (11)
Hartsdown Technology College

MY HARTSDOWN DAY

H   istory is fun
A   rt must be done
R   E is delightful
T   echnology is a handful
S   cience is stressful
D   rama is great
O   K
W   e're done
N   ow let's have some fun.

Rochelle Mandeville (11)
Hartsdown Technology College

SLEEPYHEAD

It's time to get out of bed,
Which I hate because I'm a sleepyhead.
Getting dressed and finding my clothes,
Getting my tie stuck round my nose.
Going to school to meet my mate,
If I miss my bus I will be late.
Going to class with all my gear,
Everybody calling 'Yes Miss, I'm here.'
The first lesson seems too quick,
But as the day goes on, I tend to feel thick.
When it comes to break I'm really glad,
If I didn't have it, I think I would go mad.
English, science, games and RE,
Followed by maths and history.
When it's lunchtime, I need my food,
To keep me going and in a good mood.
Textiles, art and IT,
Followed by successmaker and geography.
When the final pips go at half past three,
Means it's time to go for you and me.
When I get home I like to rest,
But I've got to study for that test.
A load of homework all to do,
Will this day ever be through?
At last I've done, I can go to bed,
Which I love because I'm a sleepyhead.

Portia Godden (11)
Hartsdown Technology College

MY VERSION OF WILLIAM BLAKE'S 'THE SCHOOL BOY'

I love to wake on a summer's day
When the sun shines in my eyes
I can go down the beach
And eat ice cream all day
Oh what a great feeling to eat cold ice cream.

But to go to school on a summer's day
It makes me feel so sad
The teachers act so mean and evil
And the Year 7s spend all day outside
Running around and playing football
Looking like they love their lives
With no cares in the world.

When I'm there I don't want to stop
And worry about a thing
I can't enjoy playing that much
When I know I have to go back there
I can't do what I want to do with my life
It makes me so depressed.

How can we be expected to go to school
Five days a week?
Or how can we live our lives?
Why must we obey the teachers' orders
And do it on demand?
It makes us feel so sad!

Christopher Lane (15)
Hartsdown Technology College

137

BULLYING IS . . .

Like an unfathomable maze, it's never-ending,
Like a never-ending journey down an alleyway,
Like a nasty day, that keeps on going,
Like a heart, it never stops,
Like a never-ending nightmare,
Like a wart that is always there,
Like a hole that goes on forever.

Janine Judd (13)
Hartsdown Technology College

BULLYING IS . . .

Like an unfathomable maze, it's never-ending,
Like an unfortunate clock, it's like a time lock,
Like a no way out situation,
Like a cave where you're trapped,
Like a place you can't get out from,
Like a room on your own where no one is there to comfort you.

Donna Lehan (14)
Hartsdown Technology College

BULLYING IS . . .

Like a door closing on you and won't open again,
Like a ton of bricks falling on you and you can't get them off you,
Like a shadow you can't get rid of,
Like an unfathomable maze which never ends,
Like a past you cannot forget, it plays on your mind,
Like a chain you cannot get out of.

Martin Ventham (13)
Hartsdown Technology College

LIL HAMSTER @ TALK21.COM

In an old summer field
Where it was not summer anymore
Where my love was once to build,
But then I saw
Saw, my love to be.

As we walked through the autumn breeze
We felt the tingling of the falling leaves
The leaves were orange, red and brown
As they fell to the dirty ground.

The night started to draw in
As I gave him the biggest grin
I gave him a kiss to last all night
As we held each other very, very tight.

Chanelle Stevens (13)
Hartsdown Technology College

BULLYING IS . . .

Like a knife through someone's heart,
like a killer waiting to kill you,
like a wasp stinging you all over,
like a tiger hungry for food,
like a thunderstorm destroying everything
in the way,
like a mother telling the child off,
like a stampede with elephants and hippos
hitting and running all over you.

Jessica Blake (13)
Hartsdown Technology College

BULLYING IS . . .

Like stabbing someone continuously in the back,
like an elephant stamping on a fly,
painful, like losing a close family member,
like a cat trying to escape the claws of a dog,
like being in a cell that you can't escape from,
like a piece of string that may never end,
like cancer that's hard to get rid of.

James Walker (13)
Hartsdown Technology College

BULLYING IS . . .

Like acid eating through you,
like pains that you get in your stomach,
like an old sweater tossed to the side,
like dying over and over again,
like candle wax melting forever and ever,
like tears hitting the floor hard,
like smoking bashing your lungs non-stop.

David Margrave (13)
Hartsdown Technology College

BULLYING IS . . .

Like a strong river pulling you down,
like a dog fearing its owners,
like fearing a ball waiting to hit you,
like a tiger in a cage,
like waiting in a dark alley on your own,
like the fear of falling off a cliff.

Kirsty Beddows (13)
Hartsdown Technology College

MY FIRST WEEK AT HARTSDOWN

I'll always remember
The sixth of September,
Butterflies in my tum
As I said goodbye to my mum.
We all met in the hall,
My first day at senior school,
We were the new year seven,
All aged twelve and eleven.
Mrs Dalmedia was also new,
It was her first day at Hartsdown too . . .
With our timetables written,
Like all the children in Britain,
I set to my task,
With the rest of the class.
Things weren't so bleak,
On my very first week.

Stacey Tompsett (12)
Hartsdown Technology College

BULLYING IS . . .

Like a kitten having fun,
It scratches and bites until it knows what it has done.
Like a shark attack, attack, attack, attack!
When you think it's over, it comes right back.
Like an eagle chasing a brown hare,
Like a hunter that has shot a little bear.
Like a lioness chasing an antelope,
Imagine running for your life, could you cope?
A game barely anyone wants to play,
Like a tiger chasing its defenceless prey.

Mary Gonella (13)
Hartsdown Technology College

SCHOOL CHANGES WEIRDLY

My junior school it's so small,
I miss my old teachers,
They were so sad when we left.

My junior school,
I always took a fall,
I miss it so much,
I'm so sad and angry.

My secondary school it's so big,
I like the teachers,
They are kind.

My secondary school's full of people so big and tall,
I'm the little one now,
It happened in a flash.

I feel all grown up,
But somehow I still feel small,
The blazer, the organiser and the tie,
What's happened? Where am I?

Charlotte Perry (11)
Hartsdown Technology College

BULLYING IS . . .

Like a spike through your spine.
Like a maze you can't escape from.
Like a message that will never go.
Like a wall you can never knock down.
Like a sweet you can't swallow.
Like a rope you can never tie.

Aimee Penfold (13)
Hartsdown Technology College

BULLYING IS . . .

Like an unfathomable maze, it's never-ending.
Like a burning building, you can't get out of.
Like your own room is padlocked.
Like an animal pinning you to the ground.
Like a bottomless pit.
Like a great sword lashing down on you.
Like a huge weight on your shoulders.
Like you're in a desert with no help.

Matthew Parker (13)
Hartsdown Technology College

SCHOOL

S   chool is the best
C   ool food
H   ard work
O   wn planner
O   nline computers
L   oads of computers which are cool.

Lawrence Wolf (11)
Hartsdown Technology College

SABRE-TOOTHED HEFFALUMP

He could eat you alive,
He has big, sharp teeth that could rip you apart in two seconds,
His body is so big and round,
He breathes a smell that could knock you out,
He is as big as two elephants,
But he wouldn't hurt a fly.

Matthew Coles (11)
Hartsdown Technology College

MY FAMILY

My dad is ill
There is no pill
And he's going blind
He's got a bit fat
He is a big brat
And he's got a big behind.

My mum, she's no fun
Because she always
Smacks my bum,
But when I'm a good boy
She will go and buy
Me a new toy.

My grandad he's so funny
He also is my grandma's honey
He goes to work in a car
Because he has to travel far.

My nan she's the apple of my eye
And when she goes to Spain, I'll cry,
But she is still here
Buying me lots of gear.

My brother he's a twit
He throws a fit
If he's in a mood
And also when he has the
Wrong food.

This is all my family
I hope that they all love me!

Aaron Arniszewski (11)
Hartsdown Technology College

BULLYING

I often hear them talking,
Saying horrible stuff about me.
They make me feel like walking
Off a cliff, way out at sea.

I scream and cry,
But they don't go away.
I always ask myself why
They keep hurting me each day.

I wonder why they hate me,
But the answer's just not clear.
What's wrong with me, I can't see,
But telling is what I fear.

It's not as though they punch and kick me,
Or throw stones at my face.
The pain you cannot see,
People would say it's a disgrace.

But they won't leave me,
They'll haunt me for the rest of my life.
When I'm at work or with my family,
They'll still be tearing me up with a knife.

So when you turn to a so-called friend
And hurt and bully them,
Remember what it felt like for me,
It felt like the horrible end.

Florence Gentle-Spens (13)
Hartsdown Technology College

SUMMER TO AUTUMN

Summer's nearly gone,
Summer's almost over,
Flowers start to slowly disappear
And trees start going orange, yellow, red.

No more splashing in the sea,
No more lying on the sand,
No more eating ice creams
And no more sunbathing.

No need for sunglasses or suntan lotion,
Pack your little tops and shorts away,
Now the sun has gone away.

Kerry Vella (13)
Hartsdown Technology College

FRIENDSHIP

F   riendship is very important to me,
R   eally good friends are what I have,
I   like nearly everyone in my class,
E   veryone has a friend,
N   obody is alone,
D   oes everyone know this?
S   urely you do,
H   owa, Becky, Charlotte, Jo, Rachel, Ruth,
I   mportant to me,
P   recious friendship is what we have.

Hayley Taylor (12)
Hartsdown Technology College

HARTSDOWN TECHNOLOGY COLLEGE

H artsdown is the best of schools
A lways difficult work, getting harder all the time
R eading in the library improves your vocab
T he half term gives you a break
S cantek is outstanding and fun
D ance and drama is sometimes fun
O h school is the only way to learn
W e receive merits and gotchas if we do good
N ever mind if you get lost, people will help you.

Ben Akhurst (11)
Hartsdown Technology College

SCHOOL TESTS

Going to school
Get into class,
Need to do a test,
I hope I pass.

Pen and pencil,
All set up,
Need some water
In a cup.

It's all over now,
I'm so relieved,
Hope I've done my best,
The best I can achieve.

Michael Atkins (12)
Hartsdown Technology College

GARLINGE

G arlinge was my favourite school
A ll the teachers were really cool
R un around break and lunchtime
L eaving the work but getting in on time
I was really good, in fact quite clever
N ot given a detention, ever!
G oing out on trips was really good
E specially the day we went to the wood.

Richard Lane (11)
Hartsdown Technology College

THE HEDGEHOG

It has got spikes like rusty nails for its defence,
It has a brown button nose for sensing out its food,
It has got a good camouflage when it is in the dark.

Scott Francis (11)
Hartsdown Technology College

HARTSDOWN

H urrying to Hartsdown
A rriving at nine
R ushing through people
T o get there on time
S itting in the classroom
D oodling on a book
O ut of the window
W e stare and look
N ow at 3.30, bag off the hook.

Ricky Davies (11)
Hartsdown Technology College

THE SUN

He needs his shiny bright body
To brighten the Earth and the night-time sky,
He looks like a great big ball of fire floating in the sky,
He reacts immediately when you touch him.

He works like an alarm clock blazing through the curtains and
waking you up,
He grows flowers and crops making the world beautiful,
He shines straight into our pupils and allows us to see,
A gigantic £1 coin in the sky that we couldn't do without.

Richard Pownall (11)
Hartsdown Technology College

BULLYING IS . . .

Imprisonment like a lion in a cage,
Is painful as if a young child's dying slowly,
Like being lost in a huge mirror maze,
Like a recurring cold,
Like a snake poisoning you.

Saima Yousuf (14)
Hartsdown Technology College

BONFIRE NIGHT

On Bonfire Night the guy is set alight,
With a crimson fire that burns so bright,
The fireworks explode with all their might,
The smoke drifts up into the night.
Hooray for Bonfire Night.

Abigail Faulkner (12)
Hartsdown Technology College

LIES

In this war we have no fun
Killing fathers and killing sons.
The mothers at home cry for their kin,
Because of leaders creating sin.

The tired soldiers keep marching on,
While innocent people hide from the bombs.
In these wars who's to blame?
It doesn't matter, we're all the same.

Fighting for pride or fighting for greed,
All war does is make countries bleed.
The soldiers fight on despite the pain,
Through the thunder of guns and the rain.

They said war was great but that's a lie,
Fighting,
Killing
And having to die.

Ben Catt (15)
Hartsdown Technology College

HARTSDOWN

H artsdown is great, Hartsdown is fun
A nd you want to come here
R un riot and have fun
T eachers are strict
S o are the students
D on't want to mess with 'em
O h it's great here
W ow, you would really like it here
N ow I have to go. Goodbye.

Nicole Grant (11)
Hartsdown Technology College

A DAY IN OUR SCHOOL

H appy children everywhere
A nnoying teachers
R otten boys all over the place
T imid little girls
S ome boys act so silly
D own the corridor of shame
O utside Mr Lippitt's office
W indows everywhere
N ever looking in, but out

T otally boring lessons
E very day, in every way
C ool isn't the word for
H aving lessons *every* day
N othing can explain that
O ther lessons can be good
L ike cooking, tech and all sorts
O bnoxious children all over the place
G etting on with the day is all I want
Y es, yes, I'm going home

C an I just leave this place?
O pen 24 hours a day
L aughter never is here
L aughter is only on good days
E very day I say this
G ritting my teeth
E very day bearing with it.

Ruth Stone (12)
Hartsdown Technology College

MY FIRST DAY AT SECONDARY SCHOOL

Secondary school, secondary school,
The first day was pretty cool.
All I wanted to do was sleep,
My old school clothes in a bundled heap.
I got up and walked to the door,
I did not feel childish anymore.

I put on my trousers and a shirt
And my shoes, they really hurt.
My mum said I looked smart,
That gave me a good start.
I found my blazer too big,
I was ready to go to a gig.

At 10 to 9 I got to school
And made my way to the hall.
We all got sorted into our forms,
(They have massive lawns.)
Soon we were in our lessons,
Getting letters for dance sessions.
I fit in now.

Ella Chapman (11)
Hartsdown Technology College

SCHOOL

Children going in and out
Hear them scream, hear them shout
Some of them are very violent
When they've gone, it's very silent

Lessons going on and on
Why do they always take so long?
Most of them are very boring
The teacher nearly finds us snoring

When it's lunch, it's a long queue
When it's gone, it's about half-two
We have to follow lunchtime rules
The smell of lunch makes you drool

I've gone home, I'm so glad
I hang up my coat and bag
Then put my blazer on a hanger
Then I raffle in my planner.

Katrina Marney (11)
Hartsdown Technology College

MY FIRST WEEK AT HARTSDOWN

That's it,
No more freedom.
I just want to think and sit,
I'm scared of what they'll do,
All the older kids,
I'm kind of scared of them, are you?

My lessons are kind of . . .
How can you say it,
They're exciting is the only word
I can think of!
The teachers, they're nice,
They tell you where to go.

I like school,
It's not that bad,
Work is not that hard,
Work is kind of fun.
I like school,
It's better than I thought.

Carina Banham (12)
Hartsdown Technology College

ST SAVIOUR'S GOOD AND BAD

Playing on the fields on hot summer days,
Staring out the window always in a gaze.

Teachers moaning and shouting at me!
I wish I was at home and thrown away the key.

The thing I hated most was PE,
Especially when I fell over and bruised my knee.

My uniform was cool,
But now it is too small.

We were year 6 making a big, loud noise,
Leaving behind our junior school toys.

Playing 'had' was my favourite sport,
Lucky for me, I never got caught.

I was a devil, never was good,
Down at the head's office I always stood.

Soon was the day,
When I was on my way,
Off to big school,
At last.

Hooray!

Emily Newman (11)
Hartsdown Technology College

WAR

Innocent citizens become victims of war,
It is never the rich, it's always the poor.
War is everywhere, everybody affected.
It's like a disease, it makes them infected.

I think war should not have begun.
How could people win? Not think of lives lost and describe war as fun?
People cannot forget the traumas of war
Because it never stops and tomorrow there could be more.

Michael Fay (14)
Hartsdown Technology College

THE SCHOOL BOY

I love to wake on a summer's day,
When the sun shines bright.
I can go to the beach
And have some fun.
Oh, what a great feeling to run
Around and have some fun.

But to go to school on a summer's day
It is all hot and boring, it makes me feel angry.
The teachers act so smart, it gets on my nerves -
And the Year 7s spend the day at the swimming pool
Looking for trouble.

When I'm there I try to swim
And not to worry about my bad thoughts,
I can't enjoy swimming because I get mobbed by kids,
I can't do anything,
I just don't want to fight.

How can we be expected to go to school and just listen,
Or be expected to write and do work?
Why must we be bored to death
And be made to work hard?
It makes us all so hot and bothered.

Michael Lambert (14)
Hartsdown Technology College

MY FIRST WEEK AT HARTSDOWN

Hartsdown school is close and near,
My first week I had a fear.
Was I right or was I wrong
To pick this school? I had no idea.
Now I'm here, the truth can be told,
I like the school, till I'm 16 years old.

Kate Hearsey (11)
Hartsdown Technology College

BULLYING IS . . .

Like a past you can't forget reflecting back in your mind,
Like a venomous snake that won't let go,
Like your worst nightmare,
Like needles piercing your body all over,
Like bruises covering your body,
As if they're right to do this, *they are wrong!*

Sarah Greves (13)
Hartsdown Technology College

BULLYING IS . . .

Like a fire always burning,
Like a shadow always following,
Like a storm that keeps raging,
Like a cobweb you can't escape from,
Like a pain that's always there,
Like a plague of rats,
Like a hurricane.

Stacey Nicholls (13)
Hartsdown Technology College

IN THE GYM

Girls and boys twisting and turning,
You and me watching and staring,
Many children leaping about,
Neat work without a doubt.
After gym we are dying of thirst,
Straddle on the floor, lets me get first.
Time's running out, must finish soon,
I jumped so high, I almost touched the moon.
Calm and quiet in the gym,
Then screams and cheers come from the crowds.

Michaela Hawkins (13)
Hartsdown Technology College

MY OLD SCHOOL

My class was nice,
It was so big,
The walls were yellow,
The chairs were big,
My school was nice,
The walls were yellow,
The hall was big,
My teacher was nice,
Her hair was short,
She had glasses,
She always gave out prizes.

Jade Thrumble (11)
Hartsdown Technology College

THE BULLIES

I wake up scared and worried,
I call down to my mum
'Do I have to go to school today?'
The reply is 'Yes.'
As I get dressed, a tear rolls down my cheek,
As I walk down my road the nasty names come back to me.
When I walk through the square to my form room
I think it's all going to be fine.
Then across the square a year nine shouts a nasty name,
I say to myself
Why me? Why me?
This bullying must stop.
I go to my first lesson,
Get crushed in the corridor.
Get in the door,
No names so far.
Maybe on the way to lesson two,
I'm standing right next to the door.
There, he is saying nasty things,
Why me? Why me?
This bullying must stop.

Lauren Miles (11)
Hartsdown Technology College

BULLYING IS . . .

Like a shadow you can't escape,
Like a really bad toothache,
Like being chased in a dream,
Like a brother, you see him every day,
Like a part of yourself, it's always with you.

Stephen Stroud (13)
Hartsdown Technology College

SCHOOL BOY

I love to wake on a summer's day
When I can eat chocolate
And go to play
When the sun is shining in the sky
I can go to the cinema and get some popcorn
Oh what a great feeling inside.

But to go to school on a summer's day
It makes me want to cry
The teachers think they're hard
And it makes me feel like I'm sinking in lard
And the Year 7s spend the day outside playing games
Looking for trouble in a dirty puddle.

When I'm there I don't have a care in the world
And I worry about my freedom
My friends and how the day is going to end
I can't enjoy doing what I want to do when I'm stuck
In school doing something boring
I can't do anything on my own
My life is such a groan
I just don't want to do anything
So please let me go home.

How can we be expected to be happy inside where it is cold
And to do boring work that makes me break down and cry?
Why must we be stuck in here
When it is nice and hot outside
And the birds are singing?
It makes us all so mad.

Michelle Male (14)
Hartsdown Technology College

SECONDARY SCHOOL

First day at secondary school,
I looked like a fool.
Everyone staring in the playground,
It was loud and full of sound.
Walking to my first session,
Only to find there were six more lessons.
Getting stuck in the corridor,
Went back for more and more.
I once got lost on my way,
Then I found my friend, May.
I didn't know what to do,
So I went off to find you.
Standing there on my own,
I was all alone.
Waiting for my meal,
On a steep, steep hill.
I was glad to get home,
So I could use the phone.

Sophie Healy (11)
Hartsdown Technology College

ENGLISH LIGHT

Throughout the fiery forest of hell
Honour and pride will reign supreme.

Wherever there is evil
The English flag will take over.
Where there is death
A rose will take its place.

Patriots who believe for their country
It will only be the beginning.

Mark Page (14)
Hartsdown Technology College

FIRST DAY NERVES

First day nerves at secondary school,
Everyone staring, you feel like a fool.

Walking around the big, scary playground,
Your back is burning with the whispering sound.

Find out that your teacher's the best,
Then she tells you it's time for a test.

Walk to the hall, your heart is beating,
All the new people that you'll be meeting.

In you go for another lesson,
You don't know what it is, a fun or boring session.

School is scary, you just want to go home,
You don't know where you're going, you feel all alone.

It's half-past three, the pips have gone,
The day's been great but you wish it wasn't so long.

Laura Mitchell (11)
Hartsdown Technology College

HARTSDOWN

H aving to wear a tie most of the time,
A rriving at 8.45
R unning and screaming to get to the lesson
T ime to go to the next lesson
S inging in a band
D oing homework so it's done
O ver 80 classrooms
W alking and running
N ever liked this school.

Aaron Rushton (14)
Hartsdown Technology College

BUTTERFLY

Its spots and lines will turn your mind,
You might actually wish you were this colour,
It flies in the sky,
Up, up and away it goes into the deep blue sky.
Caterpillars transform into this wonderful creature,
Flapping its wings.

Abby Saunders (11)
Hartsdown Technology College

FOOD

F   ood, food, fantastic, frustrating when it's gone
O   h I love food,
O   lives, omelettes, oh so lovely, I like them
D   elicious.

Andrew Lockyer (11)
Hartsdown Technology College

WAR POEM

They went with songs marching about the roads and dirt tracks.
They fell to the ground with the foe.
They sang war songs hoping they would come back.
They did come back but not as the men they were.

Andrew Blackburn (14)
Hartsdown Technology College

TEACHERS

T eachers are nice sometimes, but not when they are in a bad mood.
E very day I see my form tutor who is nice
A nd my English teacher is really great too as she gives us merits.
C olouring in electronics is fun with my tech teacher.
H eadteacher walks around watching in our lessons and seeing
if we're good.
E ating lunch in the hall, the canteen or in our form rooms.
R eading books when we have finished our work.
S till working at 3.30 sometimes because of the naughty boys.

Natalie Moore (11)
Hartsdown Technology College

HARTSDOWN DAYS

H appy to be here
A nd I love English
R E is great
T echnology is the best
S chool is fun, I learn something new every day
D etentions are bad
O ut of classroom, ready for lunch
W aiting to be served takes awhile
N ow it is time to go home.

D oing homework is always fun
A fter school I have my tea
Y es, I am going to school tomorrow.

Lauren Lipscomb (11)
Hartsdown Technology College

HARTSDOWN

H artsdown is cool,
A nd so is this poem,
R eading is good for you,
T eachers meet you in the classrooms,
S ometimes I find it boring,
D on't swear anywhere,
O ut of the classroom, ready for lunch,
W hen the pips go, it's the end of lunch.
N ow it's time to go home!

I t's time to go to open day,
S uccessmaker is what I'm doing.

C an I create a good impression to make the children come here?
O h no! They are walking this way,
O h I don't know what my score was,
L ast thing to do, switch off the computer and go home.

Nicholas Haynes (11)
Hartsdown Technology College

HARTSDOWN SCHOOL

H aving to do work
A ll questions right
R eading books from the library
T elling the teacher about the bully
S itting down
D oing time in detention
O wing the dinner lady 50p
W riting homework in my planner
N ow I'm a big boy wearing a blazer and tie.

Ryan Riddell-Broomfield (11)
Hartsdown Technology College

MY BEST FRIEND MICHAEL AND HIS FAMILY

Michael is really cool
He likes going to the swimming pool
All day long he has good fun
And also makes fun for everyone
He doesn't really like his brother at all
Especially when they go to the same school
Every day he strokes his dog
And in the afternoon he takes her for a jog
His sister is really rotten
Sometimes he wishes she was forgotten
His mum and dad are really kind
Parents like these are hard to find
This is why Michael's my best friend
We'll be friends right to the end.

Philip Quigley (11)
Hartsdown Technology College

CAT POEM

Cats are sleek and beautiful,
Their eyes glow in the dark.
In the day they guard their grounds,
So other cats should keep clear.
They love to lay in the warm sun
As a human strokes their fur.
They eat the food that humans give them,
But also they catch their prey.
In the night when you're asleep
The cats go out to play.

Sheryl Martin (11)
Hartsdown Technology College

DOLPHINS!

Dolphins are fun,
Dolphins are kind,
Dolphins are cuddly,
Dolphins are happy.

Dolphins,
Dolphins are playful,
Dolphins like balls,
Dolphins like to play all night.

The best things of all,
They play like puppies and kittens.

Samantha Overy (11)
Hartsdown Technology College

LOSS

As I stand time passes ever onwards,
But time is not my master anymore,
You are gone and now there is no forwards.
Chaos and confusion heed to no laws.
I catch the air and press it to my face,
Remembering how once it held your breath
And look at you, and in your eyes can trace
Your memories of life, now clasped in death.
There is no joy, I have forgotten fear.
Emotions can be scattered far afield.
Music falls unheeded upon my ear
Because the cry inside me will not yield.
Love is a fickle friend, as love's words spoken.
Promised love forever; promise broken.

Fiona Scoble (15)
Highworth Grammar School

ROCK MONSTER

There's a rock by the Severn bridge,
It looks down at the sea,
With glowing amber eyes
Embedded in stone.
The Earth shakes as he yawns,
A cave filled with diamond teeth appears,
Glistening.
Coal feet beneath the surface,
Pull upwards,
Breaking through earth.
Great cracked arms reach towards the sky,
Longing with a heart of marble to be released.
Slowly turning his face away,
The eyes of light close,
Drifting
To sleep,
Then free.

Clare Hammond (12)
Highworth Grammar School

FLINT

No choice but to let the tide wash over me,
Let it rush through my veins and my entire body.
Knowing that the boiling blood will never cool,
Taking over my body, passion overwhelming me.
Writhing through my soul as the passion takes control.
Let the heat take over or suffer in burning flames,
Nothing can stop the Fire, body not the same.
I knew I could feel the heat, knew I could feel its power,
Only you hold the flint and only you can douse the fire.

Samantha Smith (16)
Highworth Grammar School

THE ZODIAC

The zodiac - Aries - a ram,
His horns curve into the words of you future.

The zodiac - Taurus - a bull,
The bell through his nose jingles the tune of what the stars say.

The zodiac - Gemini - twins,
A double chance of receiving or losing what is written in the stars.

The zodiac - Cancer - a crab,
His nipping claws grab the fortune-telling stars.

The zodiac - Leo - a lion,
His tremendous roar tells you what the stars say.

The zodiac - Virgo - a virgin,
Her lonely heart beating the syllables of your future.

The zodiac - Libra - a balance,
Your horoscope evenly displayed across the scales of perfect balance.

The zodiac - Scorpio - a scorpion,
Writing your future with its deadly poison.

The zodiac - Sagittarius - an archer,
His arrows leave a trail of writing - your horoscope.

The zodiac - Capricorn - a goat,
His bleating calls are your future.

The zodiac - Aquarius - a water-bearer,
Your horoscope shown in the arching waves.

The zodiac - Pisces - fish,
Writing your future in the golden sand of the sea.

Claire Linkins (12)
Highworth Grammar School

JACK FROST RAP

I'm Jack Frost, I'm an unseen creature,
But don't be scared cos I promise I won't eat ya,
I tiptoe round the gardens in the middle of the night,
Before anyone's awake and before it gets light,
But sometimes I finish at the crack of dawn,
So if you wake up early, you might catch me on your lawn,
But of course I'm invisible, so that would be quite silly,
But there's one thing you'll notice; that it's very, very chilly,
That's all my work that I'd done the night before,
So if I were you I wouldn't step out of that door,
'So what is he?' I hear you asking in your head,
While you're snuggled up all nice and warm in your lovely bed,
I think I'm quite attractive if I say so myself,
Although I am quite small, I don't look like an ugly elf,
OK there's one exception, and that would be my ears,
Cos they're horrible and pointy so I hide them all the year,
I use my woolly hat with the bobble on the top,
Because it's nice and warm and it hides my ugly mop,
Oh there's another thing, my brown and sticky hair,
When I brush it in the morning it just goes everywhere,
Then there's my nose, all pointy and spotty,
Fine, number three, I must be going dotty,
I'm Jack Frost, so of course I can't be suave,
I'm here to give you misery, not to make you laugh,
I make it freezing cold, and block up pipes and plugs,
But still you have your ways of being snug as bugs,
By sitting on a rug and lighting up a fire,
While I wait patiently watching the smoke rise higher,
Go on then, I lose and today you humans win,
I'll just go home, wait for tomorrow, and cook for my wife, Lynne!

Charlotte Linter (12)
Highworth Grammar School

DROP BOMBS TOMORROW

George W Bush sits at his desk in the adverse, artificial light,
Opens up his small, black book and begins to write.
He dates his page the eleventh of September, the light in the room
                                                seems to draw more dim,
As he writes two sentences then closes his book. No one, but no
                                             one gets one over on him.

All about the country that night an impenetrable smog of despise,
Clogs up people's brains and chokes their hearts. Hate visible in
                                             each person's eyes.
And as American children cry and cry and cry in vain,
Around the other side of the world another child is in pain.

The Afghan child knows only its empty stomach, which growls
                                             and grumbles away,
Of course this innocent child can't control and does not know the
                                            other horrors of that day.
And yet the western world with their war against 'Terror',
Do not think what could happen to this child if they make an error.

For humans could make mistakes when an area is being missiled,
And bombs do not choose victims. They don't distinguish between
                                             'enemy' and 'child'.
But, alas, no matter. The deed must be done,
In order for the scores to go up; Taliban 1 - America 1

And in his daily planner 2001. In a black, noxious pen labelled sorrow,
The President of the USA wrote 'Shed tears today. Drop bombs
tomorrow'.

Laura Pizzey (13)
Highworth Grammar School

I WOULD BE LIKE IT

I watched a giraffe go galloping by upon one summer's morn,
When a wonderful, exciting thought inside head did dawn.
I would act like it,
I would think like it,
This animal I would be
And no longer could anyone, hate or dislike me.
Time went very quickly when this plan was about to start,
When across my stony, dry path did a fast, slim cheetah dart.
I would act like it,
I would think like it,
This animal I would be
And no longer could anyone, hate or dislike me.
Being a fast, slim cheetah was not easy, more like hard,
When a small, leaping antelope came bouncing across my yard.
I would act like it,
I would think like it,
This animal I would be
And no longer could anyone, hate or dislike me.
Being a small, leaping antelope was not easy on my feet,
When another fascinating animal came wandering down my street.
It acted like me,
It thought like me,
This animal I could be,
Then I realised that this creature was actually one of me!

Rachael Abbott (13)
Highworth Grammar School

AUTUMN DAYS

The skies are filled with fleeing birds,
The grass is wet with dew.
The leaves are scattered on the ground,
The sky's a hazy blue.

The flowers crumple in the cold,
Nipped by the frosty air.
The sun seems much more distant now,
It's lost its summer glare.

The spider webs are chains of pearls,
The drops shine in the sun.
The hedgehogs find their winter homes,
Their sleeping has begun.

The squirrels run up and down the trees,
They hope to hide their food
And all in all the woodland scene,
Is in an autumn mood.

A hazy sun, a crimson sky,
A frost rests in the air.
The fields are bare, the corn's now gone,
The fox sleeps in his lair.

Then the night with darkened sky,
So clear and flecked with stars,
Yet with each day the winter comes
And autumn must depart.

Sarah Worsley (14)
Highworth Grammar School

THE ZODIAC BOY!

There is going to be a Zodiac boy,
With his own travelling ship
And he will have a space slug
And its name will be Rip Chip.

His mum is a cyborg
And his dad is a bee,
But he will be genetically processed,
From his parents 'boy design' decree.

His robot bedroom will be amazing,
With a bed that makes itself
And because the house is a vacuum,
There won't be dust on the porthole or shelf.

His grandfather lives on 'Danger Zone',
It's a planet called 'XX23'.
He wants to see Zodiac every week
And he will give him sweets for free.

Whatever he wants from his parents,
Like a planet or a moon of his own,
He will get like a flash because he is special
And his future is already sewn.

I have given you visions of Zodiac boy
And what fabulous visions they are,
But he won't be born until three thousand and three,
But for the time being I give you . . .
Horoscope boy!

Charliene Keen (12)
Highworth Grammar School

MEMORIES

Walking upon an old dirt track,
Looking upon a rainbow stream,
I see a young boy playing there,
But he cannot see me.

I watch him paddle icy feet,
Happy face glowing like a winter moon,
Rolling on the mossy banks,
But I know that he will be gone soon.

I see him run like a racing horse,
Past churches that no longer stand,
I see his mother calling him,
Waving a once-again young hand.

He plays on lush, green meadows,
Where now houses are,
He plays without knowing it, through their doors,
The walls are to him no bar.

I see him, though others are blind to it,
He casts no shadow in the morning sun,
I smile sadly at memories I can see,
For I can remember, that this boy was -
Me.

Anna Fodor (12)
Highworth Grammar School

THE BATTLE

I am walking down the side street,
My sister walking with me,
I was deliberately whistling an annoying tune,
I wanted to get on her nerves.

It didn't look as if I was winning,
Her face was still as solid as a brick,
Her nose was poised upright,
It was going completely wrong.

I started walking quicker,
I wanted to leave her behind,
But no, she kept right up with me,
Another technique was needed.

I knew by now that I was going downhill,
But then to my surprise she vanished down the other street,
Whilst I walked down the norm,
Well then who had won?

Was it me
Or
Was it her?

Claire Cartwright (12)
Highworth Grammar School

GRIEF

Let the skies turn crimson and black
And let fears and nightmares rule the Earth
For cruel death and torment stand back to back
And the soulless ravens cackle with callous mirth.
Never again will I feel blessed sun
As the dying rays in the sky I chase
As the world's stopped and nightmares have begun;
Everywhere they torture me with your face.
Since they tore you from my grasp,
Demons enclose me with their tattered wings
And brutally to my bosom they clasp
The last picture of you, dead with my sins,
But I feel your soul resides with me
Never could they make our love die with thee.

Emma Murray (15)
Highworth Grammar School

THE CAT

As the sleek cat's green headlamps glided around
at the white blanket around him,
his moonlit stride struggled over mountains of
snow in the street,
leaving ash pawprints behind in the moonlight.

Then a graceful leap was guided to a glittering icy sill
and a whine filled the depth of the night,
a howling screech like a beginner's violin,
when people scrunch up in cosy beds.
The black cat yowls as the moon goes down.

Zana Beasley (12)
Highworth Grammar School

BABY TALK

I want food,
Everyone else is eating it,
And saying things I do not understand.
Mummy eating biscuits,
Daddy sipping tea,
There is so much food around,
Some must be spare for me!
I wave my hands upwards,
Kick my little legs,
What else can I possibly do
To fix it into their heads?
I suck my fingers,
Give a little squeal,
What other ways are there?
I simply want a meal.
Now I listen carefully to what is going on,
All the strange sounding words 'biscuit',
I try to say it, nothing happens.
'Bi . . .' Yes! Getting there.
They all look up,
'Bis . . .' They stop munching.
'Bisc . . .' A hand reaches for the plate.
Quick, I can't stop now, carry on before it's too late!
'Biscuis,' I google bouncing in my high chair.
They laugh.
Never mind, it was the best I could do,
But wait the biscuit is lifted from the plate.
'Yes Sammy,' my mummy smiled, 'that's a biscuit.'
Then she ate it.

Hermione Jones (12)
Highworth Grammar School

THE DOLPHIN

Dolphin! Dolphin!
Arching across the sea,
Who can swim as well as thee?

Dolphin! Dolphin!
Searching for prey,
Who eats better on any day?

Dolphin! Dolphin!
On the hunt,
Who gets fresher fish to munch?

Dolphin! Dolphin!
Are you scared
Of the sharks with their teeth bared?

Dolphin! Dolphin!
On the whole,
Is there anything more beautiful?

Bethany Dearlove (13)
Highworth Grammar School

BEES

In the midst of waxy shelves
An extruding hand reached in
Grasping hold of a million young
It lifted them high into the air

The cry went out
The bees readied, this was battle
Departing in a colossal swarm
Homing in on the giant enemy

The first one plunged a sting into its armour
No result, it was too well padded
On the bees rushed into a frenzy
Each one falling fatally after their attack

In the end the cause was dead
The wax returned, the honey gone
All to be spun into jars of honey
For the lives of a million bees.

James Parascandolo (14)
Langley Park School For Boys

MY AMERICAN POEM

Thousands of people working, no lie,
Two brothers standing up high,
Until a plane came out of the sky,
Boom! Great balls of fire consume the shaft,
People stared with a gasp,
Firemen speeding for help,
Not knowing what was coming from Hell.

'Help,' cried the people,
'Those men are lethal.'
Without a second to spare,
Those people are really unfair,
People evacuating door by door,
To avoid those who are breaking the US law,
The second tower went down like that,
Everyone was scared, even the cat.

Workers were working all night long,
Seeing if anyone had not yet gone.

Paul Taylor (11)
Langley Park School For Boys

THE STORM

The old fellow sat, contemplating,
In an armchair by the fire.
In front of him sat his young grandson,
Slowly beginning to tire.

'Time for bed!' He called to the boy,
Who turned and looked in dismay.
'I want a bedtime story,' he replied.
'Mum reads one to me most days.'

'OK,' the old man conceded,
Rising from his armchair.
'Pop up to bed, I'll be up in a minute,
Cuddle up to your teddy bear!'

Up the stairs the old man climbed,
Looking old and very lame.
'Read me a classic one Grandad!'
'How about The Hurricane?

In the year of '87,
16th of October was the day,
A terrible storm destroyed the south,
A storm that made others look very tame.

It caused havoc across the south,
High winds skittled down numerous trees.
The roads were blocked for miles
And houses were battered by these.

It begun on the 11th of October,
When they warned us on TV.
They told us of gale force winds,
That could endanger all and me!

The winds grew fiercer on Thursday night,
Building to a mighty climax.
Until it ferociously exploded,
Into an array of lethal attacks.

After his frightening onslaught,
The place was left in tatters,
The rebuilding job now started,
To get back to normal matters.

But six months later, the place was back
To a sense of normality.
Everything had been repaired, back the same,
But that night plagued the memory.'

The boy was now asleep,
Asleep, but still concentrating.
Enthralled within his harmless dreams,
While the old man sat, contemplating.

David Plummer (14)
Langley Park School For Boys

AMERICAN POEM

The two Twin Towers stood big and strong,
But knocking them down didn't take long.
Thousands were injured, thousands are dead.
The man who did it has 20 million on his head.
People were dying,
Bodies were flying.
The Pentagon also had a bash,
It fell to the ground with a crash.
The people in the second tower watched and waited,
For the tower to be evacuated.

Adam Jones (12)
Langley Park School For Boys

Goodwood

'Operation Goodwood', Montgomery's great plan,
Seniors and lessers wanted to break the dam.
Troop concentrations he assembled,
All around them the hard ground trembled.

One thousand Shermans here.
One thousand infantry near.
All of them ready to break cover,
Not bothered if they don't recover.

Eighty 'Eighty Eights', ready here now,
Germany's only hope, here right now.
If they lose this battle here,
They'll be running to the rear,
Never to recover,
Never to recover.

Here the British come.
Here the British come.
Like lambs to the slaughter,
They cross the water.

Now the British are over the river,
The Germans will not dither.
Will it be guns or will it be mines
That will smash the British tank lines?

The first shell screams overhead,
Ready to take off some man's head.
As it hits, the tank is destroyed,
Leaving its crew, scattered like toys.

More and more guns open up.
More and more mines blow up.
'What shall I do?' one tommy shouted,
When he realised the others had been routed.

As they retreated from whence they came,
Lead followed them back falling like rain.
It was a dreadful crossfire
And their position was dire -
But do what they could,
They knew it was futile, like the 'Hood'.

Losses were bad -
The fighting mad.
Many men lost,
For a wooden cross.

Allied propaganda mentioned no loss,
All they said was, Monty is boss.
They never showed any care,
All they did was lie from their lair.

Alas, there was no new German assault,
And, after all, it was Hitler's fault.
At the end of the war,
Erwin Rommel was no more.

Isn't it terrible, that in war
Winners die,
Whilst losers lie.

Duncan Shadbolt (13)
Langley Park School For Boys

ADVERB POEM

Slowly the snake slithered across the sand,
Slowly the submarine sank in the sea,
Slowly the scooter slid in the house,
Slowly I dragged myself to school,
Slowly the slug leaves his silvery trail.

Russell Warner (12)
Langley Park School For Boys

THE SIGHTS OF HIROSHIMA

The sky was blue, the morning bright and sunny,
But there was a slight chill in the air.
I got up and checked if I had some money,
There was none but I did not care.

It was eight fifteen am, quite early for me
And I was not fully awake yet.
I looked in a drawer and rummaged for my car key,
Found it I cried, under a net!

I was suddenly startled by a huge light,
It was big and amazingly bright.
I turned towards it and saw the greatest sight,
It looked like a camera flashlight.

I went to my window, looked out, but saw nothing,
I waited, it seemed like forever.
I was shocked, breathing really heavily, puffing,
Could not believe the chaos, never.

I ran to the door, my life was in danger,
The smell of death reeked in the streets.
A man staggered past, blood dripping from his head,
Flocks of people, like parakeets.

God, what is going on in this world nowadays?
The carnage was an awesome sight.
Body parts flying everywhere, like gun rays,
Oh my God! What the hell is this?

I ran down the streets, not caring what was there,
All I found was bodies, bodies,
People were crawling, crawling, the sight was rare,
All over the floor, there were bodies.

I could not believe the sights I was witnessing,
The terror in children's eyes.
But I was not thinking of these catastrophes,
The Yanks had filled us full of white lies.

I was angry as hell, angry as hell,
Wanted to kill those bloody Yanks,
Slit their throats, chop their heads off, I did not care,
Go in there with huge mighty tanks.

We would get them, there was no doubt about that,
Today, tomorrow, I did not know.
But get them back for this, that I did know,
But get them back for this, that I did know.

Mark Hayzer (13)
Langley Park School For Boys

THE ROAD TO DESTINY

Barbaric troops march across the fort,
Chanting and screaming to their destiny.
The battle commences at the great port,
An injured man cries out in agony.

The commanding general bellows madly,
As a fleet of bombers attack the sky.
The nation stays watching in melody,
In the distance you hear a young girl cry.

On the mountaintop, a man stands tall,
His armour becomes stained from his blood.
This person was part of this evil maul,
Looking down to the carnage on the mud.

Bodies lay still, with a look in their eyes,
Their bodies soon were covered with flies.

Liam Norval (14)
Langley Park School For Boys

A SONNET

Her black lips sealed tight against the cool air
Like dark waves with white surf she glides of sort
Her dark angry eyes disguise and despair
Such icy glares the passers-by have caught
In which you cannot help but think it wrong
Her self-righteous hate held in abstract moors
Perhaps, in not tie with the world's death song!
Forbid to question by etiquette laws
Of people past, present and future I see
That it's time to evolve. I must confess
But who to, I'm locked out with no such key
So lost with breadcrumbs, hungry and restless
As for the girl she is but that, no less
Than frustrated at the world in distress.

Jeremy Farr (13)
Langley Park School For Boys

TUESDAY, THE ELEVENTH

The clouds come out, the sky turns grey
As the two demons come out to play
This evil will cause tremendous hate
Because of its plans to disrupt fate
The deadly monsters soar above the streets
No one knowing what they plan to meet
In two foul swoops, the twin brothers are struck
And thousands of innocent lives are taken from us
Although it is devastating as things may seem
What cannot be destroyed, is the nation's great dream.

Ian Mooney (14)
Langley Park School For Boys

TWO TWIN BROTHERS

Two twin brothers once stood proud
Amongst the midst of New York's clouds
Tales and myths have all been told
But nothing can defeat the eternal cold
Loved ones lost
Count the cost
Straight from Hell came this death and woe
The first one gone crashing low
Leaving people dying in pain
Rescuers' efforts all in vain
Moments later came down his friend
Brothers forever no one to tend
Neither left standing arm to arm
No one left to harm
New York's skyline will never be the same
Explanations were all so lame.

William Bishop (11)
Langley Park School For Boys

TRAGEDY

The Twin Towers once stood proud in the centre of New York
Until one plane ploughed into one of the towers
Then the other tower was destroyed by another plane
To everyone's surprise the first tower was gone
And New York was left covered in dust
Then the people realised that their loved ones were gone
Now the Afghans were full of fear
They didn't know what was going to happen to them
They shed a tear
This Tuesday afternoon will never be forgotten.

Andrew Botten (12)
Langley Park School For Boys

WAITING

Sitting at home waiting for the letter,
Good news, we hope, will be in its content,
Hoping our dad will be for the better,
As the postman walks down the drive, the scent
Of lavender sweetens his bitter stroll,
Three hard knocks on our solid, oak door came,
It started with: Your husband did enrol,
The letter continued and said his name,
Mr Robert St Claire did die today,
His performance was probably the best,
At the memorial he does now lay,
We must now hope and pray that he does rest
In peace and harmony, God bless his soul,
He has brilliantly fulfilled his role.

Joseph Aswani (14)
Langley Park School For Boys

THE HUNTER

He stalks slowly towards his prey,
Remaining concealed from the sight of his most sought-after prize,
Inconspicuous, staying hidden away,
Keeping the oh so precious element of surprise,
He draws nearer, small beads of sweat cross his forehead,
He swallows hard,
His legs feel like lead,
He musters up his courage and moves closer still,
The short subtle movements requiring incredible will,
But he knows that what is to come,
Is indeed truly worthy of what must be done,
So that he may now finally get the chance,
To ask the girl of his dreams for just one dance.

Matthew Hutchinson (13)
Langley Park School For Boys

WAR

Death is the ultimate sacrifice to make,
To do that just for the sake of war's plot,
Causes many deaths and makes the heartache.
The stench of chaos, blood making the rot,
Insignificant over someone's fame
Or maybe not. The pain that is felt just
Does not compensate for war - a game
Played between countries because someone cussed.
The fire of a gun signifying death,
Is all overcome supposedly when won.
The last dying moment of a breath,
The way is happy for the winner's mum,
Though terrible for the loser's scars,
Is war really worth fighting just for gold bars?

Sean Fabri (13)
Langley Park School For Boys

DESTRUCTION

As the plane went charging in,
The deaths of people were soon to begin.
The flames went in like Niagara Falls,
Burning everything through the doors.

The second went soaring in,
Destroying all, for the second time.
You couldn't believe,
All the distant screams.

But now we're at war
And we hope there won't be more.

Edward Newman (11)
Langley Park School For Boys

PAIN BY TRAIN

I grab the rope and stumble into the rain,
I start to wonder 'Have I lost my mind?'
Heading forward, imagining the pain,
Feeling like I have suddenly gone blind.
Our love used to be new and very fresh,
Then I see her with another male,
All I'm thinking is the train and my flesh,
I will die because of a female.
I reach the track and onto it I jump,
With the rope I tie myself to the track
The train is coming, I can hear it, *thump,*
It's all over, there is no turning back.
I knew the man she was with at the weekend,
Oh dear, it was only her college friend.

Jack Stevens (13)
Langley Park School For Boys

LOVE POEM

Love is a warm ice cube slipping down my spine.
Love is when I get a look at your face,
But the heavy air drags me away from you.
Love is the dark daylight,
Blinding me from your pretty face.
Love is when your face gets into view,
It's like watching a fish walk.
Love is a valuable penny.
Love is when my heart feels like burning ice,
That reminds me of your face.

This cruel kindness
Splits us apart forever too long.

Aaron Sparkes (12)
Langley Park School For Boys

SONNET OF WAR AND BATTLE

You say goodbye to your woman who's fit,
You mount your weapons and your sharpened spear,
When you're in battle your belly is split,
The wound you have picked up is quite severe.
You go on horseback at a steady trot,
Or in a tank unlike times of Romans,
Because protection was low if you got shot,
Bang goes a shell and creates an explosion.
Across the floor lay guns, swords and daggers,
Soldiers lay in the ground that is muddy,
Up pops a man who can't walk, so staggers,
His face is scratched and body bloody.
At the end, we are grateful to be living,
But some years later, on goes the killing.

Michael Blair (13)
Langley Park School For Boys

DISASTER

Alarm rings a normal day,
I'm in America here to stay.
Get up, get dressed, feeling good,
The sun is rising just as it should.
Eight o'clock approaching nine,
Could be late, cutting it fine.
Emerge from subway see the light,
And there I see a dreadful sight.
A plane flies low near the tower,
Pinpoint aim, immense power,
Glass breaks and people cower.
Our lives have changed . . .

Anthony Pike (12)
Langley Park School For Boys

THE GHOST

There was a tremendous knock at the door,
And the very old ceiling started crumbling,
There was a long creak on the wooden floor,
While the furniture continued tumbling,
All of a sudden there were five loud taps,
Then the glass of 'Red Label' whisky spilled
And straight after cold air emerged from gaps,
The next thing was the entire room was chilled,
Then there was a huge bang! She was dead,
There were masses of thick red blood everywhere,
Then a large rolling thing emerged - a head!
Everyone was in for a very big scare,
The grim ghost of ghastly Gum Manor
Had returned with his twelve inch spanner.

Asanka Weeratunge (13)
Langley Park School For Boys

THE END OF THE WEEKEND

A pile of homework left untouched,
Songs of praise,
Looming Monday,
I hate Sunday!
The weekend's over,
The week awaits,
Gloomy Monday,
I hate Sunday!
The weather's bad,
Inside's moaning,
Monday's here,
Till next week,
I dread the morning.

Richard Legate (13)
Langley Park School For Boys

THE RACE

Go, go, go for the British Grand Prix,
Cars go whizzing by, shifting up and down,
Going around the track, overtaking, we can't see,
All the drivers fighting for the ultimate crown.
Fans cheering, horns honking for the winning car,
No fan knows who's going to win.
The winning driver will become a star,
Throughout the race he wouldn't have had a spin.
Bang, bang, bang, into the tyre wall,
Mika keeps crashing again and again.
This is the worst crash of all,
His next crash could be at any time. We don't know when.
The marshals runs into the scene of the crash,
Mika's OK, except for whiplash.

Daniel O'Connor (13)
Langley Park School For Boys

TWIN TERRORS

On the eleventh of September
A day that I shall always remember
One like another
Or brother to brother
They both crashed and burned

Out of the rubble
Few people had stumbled
For most people had died in the fall,
But for those who survived
It had ruined their lives
On that cursed day in New York.

Luke Richards (12)
Langley Park School For Boys

MR SOREBUM

Yesterday my dad played cricket,
He scored 17 runs and they didn't get his wicket.
But he's not as young as he used to be
And he's somewhat prone to injury.
But he tries very hard and does his best,
He just missed being picked for the Oval test.
But back to the game he played yesterday,
He didn't see the ball that was coming his way.
By the time he woke up the ball was past,
He had to get after it mighty fast.
'There he goes,' the umpire cried.
It was Grandad in disguise!
But he kept on running, he couldn't stop,
Then all of a sudden his bum went pop,
So there you have it - mighty fine.
Fancy batting No 9, 17 runs and an itching bum,
We all had a laugh, including my mum,
But cheer up Dad things can only get worse,
I hope you like my little verse.

Nick Pelling (12)
Langley Park School For Boys

NEW YORK TERROR

Two towers standing tall and proud,
They stand high above the busy New York below.
Everybody getting on with their daily life,
Working or playing, speaking or listening.

Then, suddenly without any warning,
The people watched as the first plane went in,
People in the building were working at the time,
As people in the plane were told they would die.

About 15 minutes later another plane crashed,
This time into the second tower.
Finally the two towers hit the ground,
Noisily and fiery.
Ashes covered New York like a black and grey sheet,
As firemen tried to save as many people as they could.
New York will never forget this terrible day
And we will make sure that the terrorists pay.

Jonathan Michael Roberts (11)
Langley Park School For Boys

THE TWIN TOWERS

On the 11th September
The crash began
Both the Twin Towers holding each others' hands
Side by side
Crash by crash
Both the Twin Towers were out of reach
Of each other's hands

No people to be found
Until the dogs find their ground
This day is one to remember
Mums, dads, children, all lost
We will remember their loss

The Pentagon with five sides now with 4
Who would want anymore?
Soon the war will begin
America versus Afghanistan
Who will win?

Nicholas Wakeling (12)
Langley Park School For Boys

THE DEATH OF THE TWIN TOWERS

Just another day, boring and dull
That's what I thought until about 9am

I didn't know what was happening at first
It started as a rumble and then as a roar

I was looking out my window and then . . .
I saw two planes flying at me

Then I realised I was about to die
There was only one option to run down the stairs

Running and running, I couldn't stop
Only another 20 floors to go

I was almost there when I heard a big bang
The planes must have crashed 'Oh no, I'm dead.'

I was nearly at the door when . . .
Suddenly the rubble came down.

I'd almost got out,
I'd almost survived.

Jamie Gibbons (12)
Langley Park School For Boys

WINTER'S BLESSING

During night the soft snow came,
Snowflakes gently fall without sound,
Everything seems to be floating.

Icicles hang from roofs like daggers,
The cold is stabbing through me.
Sculptures forming in the ground,
The world seems to stop and look at winter's blessing.

Light reflects to make the world ice bright
And it seems to feel like Heaven.
Everything seems to have changed,
While the wind strikes harder than before.

That was a long while ago,
Winter's blessing lessened every year
And even though the snow has left,
My body still feels cold.

Thomas McLaren (15)
Langley Park School For Boys

THE OTHER SIDE

The gleaming brilliance of moonlight on water,
Captured my brain
And took me to another world of glistening, silent figures of life.
The ground shook and shuddered with the flow of the powerful river.

Mist of silver engulfed the gnarled, twisted and decaying roots.
A single sphere of light was tattooed on the ground beside me,
It shone mysteriously flickering around with an unearthly glow.
The water trailed off into the distance,
Fish danced around my head like dreams
And the trees swayed slowly, making me dizzy,
The obscure screeching sounds of the night,
Seemed miles away from the muddy bank by the river.

Then a single shimmering droplet of water,
Slipped off a leaf,
Like a spark of silver fire.
Descending slowly it shatters,
The placid and moonlit world,
On the other side of the river.

Andrew Straiton (14)
Langley Park School For Boys

THE BALLAD OF I (A SOLDIER)

To the other side of town we must flee,
Helping to fight the enemy are we,
Up and on our way we speedily run,
Certain to die if you forget your gun.

Explosions blossom all around the roads,
Buildings collapse and so do many abodes,
Shells wreak havoc amongst our men,
I see a soldier die, I knew his name, Ken.

Stealthy to approach the line of our foe,
I scan the streets to see how far I must go,
Along my barrel I spot a German,
Pull back the trigger, I fire on a man.

Gunning down the enemy in a frenzy,
They return with furious fire at me,
Men on each side turned into bloody mounds,
We force them to retreat out of their bounds.

The chase is deadly and fast as they run,
We pursue them, I fire with my gun,
We chase and shoot until they have all fell,
We know we have sent our enemies to Hell.

We swiftly reverse back to our own zone,
Quickly we move, we hear many a moan,
We reach the other side of town once more,
The landscape has been torn by this great war.

Heaps of corpses from both armies,
For all the pride and glory, these are the fees,
The grim reaper surveys the town with glee,
I wonder if on his list there is me?

War has no winners or consolations,
There is no pride in the clashing of nations,
Just massed death and tormented tragedy,
The result of war is just casualty.

Ricky Cella (13)
Langley Park School For Boys

CRASH INTO TWIN TOWERS

C rash, bang, the towers come down
R umours of who did it were circling round
A round the world these rumours spread
S elfishness caused 1000s of deaths
H ate and anger was seen around when the towers came down

I n England there was 3 minutes' silence
N ot many survivors in the towers
T onnes of corpses in the towers
O n the ground people are scared

T uesday 11th, the day of the attack
W eeping people for all the deaths
I n America united they stand to find the terrorists against their land
N ew York the place of the attack, Manhattan to be exact

T owers down, America sad what has happened is really, really bad
O sama bin Laden the prime suspect
W hat a crime to commit
E ngland helps to clear the mess
R escue workers work day and night
S o what will happen next?

Ben McLaren (13)
Langley Park School For Boys

THE BALLAD OF THE GREAT FIRE

A lovely day in Florida,
Was not so lovely at all.
For a monster wreaked havoc upon a school,
In the classrooms, kitchens and hall.

A fire broke out in the toilets,
He tried some in the class,
But all the children escaped the school,
Except me and he was on me fast!

Trapped! With him closing in on me.
Evil smiles flickered and glowing grins jaunted.
I ran! But was chased everywhere,
Like a ghost, the fire haunted.

I ran as fast as I could, with nowhere to run,
'You'll make it out,' to myself I lied,
But in that school I could only find death,
So I cried and cried and cried.

And as if extinguishing these flames,
I found a way to the door,
A path as if Heaven out of Hell!
I raced towards that door,
But as I did some scaffold fell
And knocked me to the floor.

I lay there in dismay,
For I had lost all hope
And as I heard a voice call out,
Death grabbed me by the throat.

I could not reply, his grip was tight
And oxygen was running from me,
Hand in hand with my life,
While the fire laughed at me

And minutes later he found me,
Lying upon the floor
And brought me out into the air,
But I would breathe no more.

A lovely day in Florida,
Was not so lovely at all.
For a monster wreaked havoc upon a school,
In the classrooms, kitchens and hall.

Luke Robertson (13)
Langley Park School For Boys

THE TWO TWIN TOWERS COME TO AN END

The two Twin Towers come to an end,
Doesn't it drive you round the bend,
All this chaos taking people's lives,
Killing husbands and their wives.

All those heartless people that do not care,
All the humanity and all the despair,
All the innocent people in the towers so high,
You would never have thought they'd come to die.

All you Afghans can't you open your eyes,
All the terror it's caused, all the rubble that lies,
All the people in emotion, all the lives in theft,
Now there's the rubble only one hope left.

The two Twin Towers came to an end,
A heart-breaking moment you cannot mend,
The two Twin Towers came to an end,
Did all those lives really have to end.

Pierre Connell (12)
Langley Park School For Boys

GONE IN A DAY

It was a calm and peaceful August morn,
While travelling to work,
The streets were full of cars honking their horns
And I put on a smirk.

I entered the building and heard a sound,
Sounding like a siren,
It was screaming so incredibly loud,
Could have been a fire-on.

Falling, falling, falling down came the bomb,
There was no panicking,
Fixed on the object we stared with aplomb,
Stiff like a mannequin.

Falling, falling, falling down to the ground,
Exploding with a flash,
Creating a towering mushroom cloud,
The ceiling made a crash.

Buried under tons and tons of rubble,
Looked like Armageddon,
A once prosperous city in trouble,
All of the city gone.

Burning buildings, streets and cars everywhere,
I could not believe it,
A once prosperous city, now is air,
What was it that had hit?

I dashed home hoping my wife was okay,
I really hoped she lived,
A prosperous city, gone in a day,
Hopefully she had hid.

It was all gone, the house and the garden,
I was so horrified,
People who did this I could not pardon,
Why? Why had they all died?

Jonathan Davis (13)
Langley Park School For Boys

THE ATROCITIES IN AMERICA

Like two twin giants did they stand,
Side by side, hand in hand,
They dominated the sky,
In Manhattan for so long,
Not anymore for they have gone.

I watched the first plane nosedive down,
Into one of the towers,
I felt a shock run through my hands,
Was it a dream or was it for real?
I did not know.

About ten minutes later it happened again,
What was going on inside this troubled land?
Then I knew it was not a dream,
This was for real,
It was meant to happen.

Then the unthinkable came,
They could not take anymore,
The two once astonishing giants,
Fell to their knees
And perished forever more.

Alex Leone (12)
Langley Park School For Boys

THE BALLAD OF RYAN GURL

Someone was moving outside the window
Messing and tampering with roadworks
Damaging work, they had stooped that low
I saw their faces awash with smirks.

I called the local police force
I told them about what I'd seen
He said we'll come right away of course
I had helped keep the streets clean.

The car pulled up just outside the home
The vandals scampered right out of sight
The police went as fast as they had come,
But did not even look back or to the right.

Meanwhile three miles away Ryan Gurl
A young man of only twenty
Driving along starting to feel ill
His will to drive not plenty.

His head felt like a heavy load
He thought he would do his normal trick
And turned down the one way road
He stuck his head outside to be sick.

Then there was a nasty chink
He had cracked his head
And no longer could he think
He is a corpse, he is dead.

Liquid from where his face had been
A stain was on the tarmac
A wash of colour could be seen,
But crimson red instead of black.

Today there lays a solitary reef
Where the young man's corpse did lay
His family's lives were plunged in grief
Since two days before this day.

James Bran (13)
Langley Park School For Boys

WHO DID THIS? DID YOU?

Flash of light,
Plane in sight,
People's screams fill the air,
Terror all around.

Oh no, another,
What's it going to do?
What's that crumbling sound?
Who did this? Did you?

What's that on the news?
One hit the Pentagon,
What are we going to do?

Bin Laden did this!
How do you know?
I don't, it's just a guess.

One went for the White House,
Did the people fight and fight
Or did it get shot down on sight?

One's day's terror will soon end,
But will stay in the hearts of men,
The question still remains,
Who did this? Did you?

James Nattrass (12)
Langley Park School For Boys

THE BALLAD OF BECKET

On the 21st day of December,
She thought, 'What shall I name thee?'
As she gritted her teeth and clenched her belly,
Out of her popped he!

Thomas à Becket was he,
All the brave Christians he led,
But the King was in a blind rage,
And four kingsmen removed his head!

Educated at Merton Priory,
Thomas was destined for the church.
What an excellent child he was,
For over the Bible he did lurch.

Thomas à Becket was he,
All the brave Christians he led,
But the King was in a blind rage,
And four kingsmen removed his head!

He was appointed to be a secretary,
The secretary of Lord Pevensy.
Who inducted him to the life of a gentleman,
His father in a crisis, was he.

Thomas à Becket was he,
All the brave Christians he led,
But the King was in a blind rage,
And four kingsmen removed his head!

Thomas' life changed again in 1154,
When the new king, Henry appointed him chancellor,
I suppose it got even better, when,
Theobald thought he would be the protector.

Thomas à Becket was he,
All the brave Christians he led,
But the King was in a blind rage,
And four kingsmen removed his head!

Sadly Theobald died in 1161,
Tom then became the Archbishop man,
Tom and the King quarrelled over the church,
And for many a year the argument would span.

Thomas à Becket was he,
All the brave Christians he led,
But the King was in a blind rage,
And four kingsmen removed his head!

The King then enforced some strict laws,
Tom became unhappy as this reached his ears.
Then Tom fled the court as the King tried to charge him,
To France went he, to begin an exile of six years.

Thomas à Becket was he,
All the brave Christians he led,
But the King was in a blind rage,
And four kingsmen removed his head!

Thomas and Henry agreed to reconciliation,
But when Tom returned Henry could not stop him
From excommunicating some of his bishops
And four kingsmen overheard Henry's disgust
And from France to England they did hop.

Thomas à Becket was he,
All the brave Christians he led,
But the King was in a blind rage,
And four kingsmen removed his head!

This was the result of the kingsmen's journey,
Tom was murdered in a church,
Henry was made to bow at his tomb,
But remember, over his Bible he used to lurch.

Thomas à Becket was he,
Because of the King's dumb mistake
He is remembered by people today,
Remembered as a *saint!*

Faraz Auckbarally (13)
Langley Park School For Boys

OUTCAST

The shadow of every conversation,
The one whom everyone shuns,
The vulture that lurks around your carcass,
The victim of all your prejudiced acts,
The one you treat like a slave,
The one you torment just for fun,
The toy you abuse, again and again,
The one who endures all your beatings,
The wall that takes your insults kindly,
The creature without any emotions,
The one in the corner of every room,
The one with the misconstrued character,
The only one who really cares,
The angel who'd clip his wings for you,
The one who is there when you are in need,
The one who's treated as an outcast,
The forgiver who's always willing to forget,
The one you ignore day by day,
The only real friend you'll ever have,
The one you've treated as an outcast.

Tejus Patel (14)
Langley Park School For Boys

THE STEEL BROTHERS

The two steel brothers
Stood tall
And strong
Unbreakable.

They could stand
Wind and rain,
But their time had come
To come crashing down.

The plane is hijacked
And flown to the tower
A really good welcome
With sparks.

Many people died
The rest file for the stairs,
But halfway down
The second plane hits.

An hour later
The first building
Comes down
In a pile of dust.

Everyone else moves back
So they will not be crushed
Then the second tower
Comes flying down.

The wreckage is a pile
Of steel and glass
That is the end of
The steel brothers.

Luke Bassett (11)
Langley Park School For Boys

THE BALLAD OF THE LIGHT BRIGADE

We looked though as set to lose,
Ten hundred men on horseback came,
Nothing else we could have to choose,
Back from these men without a name.

They had us in their clutches now,
But none came to pick us off,
So soon we could retake our bows,
To the foe, we could beat them off.

We were hurt and tired, but we fought well,
Struggling forth, we took from them
Their mighty guns from the inner shell,
So they must surrender from our might.

But wait, here comes someone, but not
To once again drive us back
And from the awful guns rained shots,
As they came of life we take.

Suddenly they turn and charge,
They cannot plan to attack!
But onward they come, they barge,
But shots do not turn them back!

A wild charge, an impetuous rush,
Towards their deaths, oh the fools!
That I must destroy, kill and crush,
Men like sacks and horses like mules.

Now a few, little, now even less,
A blow can pick off at a hundred yards,
At least then, some are at rest,
To kill them all, bring all down, it is not hard.

All is over, a thousand dead,
But half of these men need not have died,
But this is what we and they did,
Not to repeat that day we have tried.

Richard Lewis (14)
Langley Park School For Boys

NEW YORK DISASTER

I was shocked when I heard the news
Help! Help!
Was it real?
Help! Help!

Aeroplanes crashing into the Twin Towers
Why? Who?
Thousands of people starting their day
Coffee and doughnuts, not today

People at bay
Do we run or do we stay?
What shall we do?

Say please to God
Let this be a dream
Flee I must
I want to survive
Screams and smoke all around

As I look back I see the building fall
Where are my friends?
I want them here
Who would do this and why?

Tom Shingles (13)
Langley Park School For Boys

THE CRASH

Busy, as everyone hurries to work
Thousands of people on the streets below,
But they didn't know
The building was to be covered in dust like snow.

In Boston terrorists were boarding planes
All terrorists carrying small knives,
When the planes did hit the World Trade Center
There was a great loss of lives.

The terrorists made a move
With their knives raised,
They shouted and called
As the attendants turned their heads and gazed.

As the first plane lined up for the World Trade Center,
The terrorists were happy and full of glee,
When the first plane went in, hundreds were killed,
It must have been an accident, how could a plane fly into the WTC?

Hurry, hurry, panic, panic,
Rubble and bodies found everywhere,
Rush, rush, disaster, disaster,
All you can hear are the injured groaning, the streets are bare.

As the second plane came,
Hatred, disaster, horror, shock,
Many stared in disbelief,
It exploded and the world did rock.

As the building came down
All hope of life is lost
Thousands have died in a short few seconds
To rebuild the WTC and bring back the lives, it would be an
                                        unimaginable cost.

Hurry, hurry, panic, panic,
Rubble and bodies found everywhere,
Rush, rush, disaster, disaster,
All you can hear are the injured groaning, the streets are bare.

Josh Mills (13)
Langley Park School For Boys

THE BIG CRUMBLE

The towers stood so high
The people inside it never knew they would die
First a plane
And then some pain

America was crying, crying, crying

The second plane came
And it was bin Laden to blame
The people gasped
And did what the firemen asked

America was crying, crying, crying

People were jumping out
What was it all about?
The world had to cry
Because they knew the people would die

America was crying, crying, crying

The hijackers would go to Hell
Because the Twin Towers fell
The fires were blazing at ten past eleven
The innocent people would go to heaven

America was crying, crying, crying.

Ravi Patel (12)
Langley Park School For Boys

A TRAGIC STORY

Patrick, the richest man I ever knew,
Cars like Jags, even a smart doorknob,
People like that man, there were very few,
He adored his work, his well-paying job.

An unbelievable sense of humour,
Very sensitive, as subtle as a tree,
Designed *major* buildings, just a rumour
And married, all this at just twenty-three.

Life was perfect, he had four great children,
Top of the world, king of all earthly men.
Behind a dreary cloud went the bright sun,
He wished that his very day had not begun . . .

Depression, from the bottom of sick hell,
Is life at the bottom of this glass of beer?
The more he drank the further he fell,
He drank down beer, along with his deep fear.

His loving kids could do nothing but cry,
O sacred alcohol, in that there bottle,
This world was cruel, he needed wings to fly,
He wanted to get away at full throttle.

And there were his wings, in a little glass jar,
Those little white pills would open the door,
The world has disappeared, gone from afar,
Patrick, slumped, lifelessly on the floor.

Suicide attempts had failed once again,
Many mental homes could not hide his pain.
Behind a dreary cloud went the bright sun,
He wished that this very day had not begun . . .

He was out with his mates having a joke,
He was on his back, he tried to be sick,
He tried to get up, he started to choke,
His life had ended in a finger click . . .

My grandpa died on that very same day,
My grandpa died in that very same way . . .

Oliver Holden-Rea (13)
Langley Park School For Boys

ARE WE?

Are we what we are,
Or are we not?
Do we see what we think we see
Walking down the street every morning?
Are they what *we* want them to be like, look like, smell like?
Is her hair blonde?
Is his hat really that awful colour?
Hasn't he been wearing that shirt for the last week?
Do we really know what's right
Or why we are what we are?
If this indeed is us!
Does Mummy always know best?
Will your eyes go square if you watch too much TV?
And is that where babies really come from?
How can ace be one *and* eleven?
Why can you never get that huge grease stain out of your trousers?
Why do birds sleep standing on one leg?
Is there a meaning to life?
Is there a meaning or a reason for anything?
Have we evolved due to fate
Or the obscure, narrow-minded psyche of one individual
Trying to play 'God'?

Alex Balbastro (14)
Langley Park School For Boys

THE TOWERS ARE DOWN

The Towers are down,
George Bush gives a frown.
Will it be war?
Will the planes soar?

Bin Laden wanted, alive or dead,
There is twenty million on his head.
Bin Laden denies,
But no one else has the supplies.

It's time to stop mourning the dead
And time to get up and raise our head.

Be brave, stand strong,
For now it won't be long.
Bin Laden will be caught
And justice brought.

Michael O'Hanlon (12)
Langley Park School For Boys

DEVASTATION

Explosions of dust in the air,
People running here and there.
Office workers trapped inside,
Never to come out alive!

Falling figures hit the ground,
Sounds that echo all around.
Debris dropping from the sky,
As the Towers say goodbye.

Tears, fire, death and smoke,
Dust so thick you nearly choke.
Men with helmets rush through the scene,
They too witness people scream.

You count the bodies, 1, 2, 3,
There lies your family.
Kneeling down with hurt and pain,
You will never see them again!

Christopher Glover (12)
Langley Park School For Boys

AMERICA

Towers crashing,
People dashing,
On that awful day.

The smoke went up,
They had run out of luck,
On that awful day.

Balls of fire,
The smoke went higher,
On that awful day.

The nation cried,
As people died,
On that awful day.

Innocent people lay on the ground,
They were never to make a sound,
On that awful day.

Joseph McCloskey (11)
Langley Park School For Boys

THE TRAGEDY ON THE 11TH SEPTEMBER 2001

Two brothers stand arm in arm,
Now it's just a metal farm.

Now as people stand and stare,
The terrorists are stripping America bare.

The Pentagon has lost a side,
As people try to run and hide.

Now as people stand and stare,
The terrorists are stripping America bare.

The emergency services working hard,
Let's hope bin Laden does get barred.

Now as the people stand and stare,
The terrorists are stripping America bare.

Us Brits stand shoulder to shoulder,
With our plans in a folder.

Now as people stand and stare,
The terrorists are stripping America bare.

The ships and planes are standing by,
Let's hope the planes won't have to fly.

Now as people stand and stare,
The terrorists are stripping America bare.

Let's hope bin Laden will give up,
Or we will have to get tough.

Now as people stand and stare,
The terrorists are stripping America bare.

I don't want this to be the end of me,
Let's hope there's not a World War III.

Paul Howes (12)
Langley Park School For Boys

A MISHAP IN MALTA

The hotel floor was made of marble,
Hard, shiny and white.
It kept guests relaxed and cool,
The glaze reflected light.

I sprinted across the slippery floor
And into a hidden edge.
My scream was heard by everyone,
As I lay across the ledge.

I managed to hobble back to my room,
Collapsing on my bed.
My parents alerted the doctor,
'Hospital,' he said.

I was lugged out to the ambulance,
By two youthful men.
My leg was strapped to a support,
The clock then struck ten.

We set off into the moonlit night,
The sirens blared loudly,
Up and down the bumpy road went,
Yet I slept soundly.

I was taken straight to the x-ray unit,
To have my leg assessed,
The doctor bellowed, 'You've fractured your leg,
So you better get some rest!'

So the nurses wrapped my leg in plaster,
Right up to my knee,
I was equipped with two silver crutches,
'Be careful,' they told me.

David Straiton (13)
Langley Park School For Boys

DARK NIGHTS

It was one dark night, when the moon was low
And a storm was brewing in the sky.
The trees were wildly blowing in the air,
The leaves were being hurled up high.

He sat there waiting, for something to come,
He knew they would be here soon.
As he sat there smoking his old ragged pipe,
Then came a loud *kaboom!*

A huge explosion, a blinding sight,
The enemies were finally here.
When will this horrible evilness stop,
After this long and dreadful year.

It was one dark night, when the moon was low
And a storm was brewing in the sky.
The trees were wildly blowing in the air,
The leaves were being hurled up high.

He stepped out front, with his gun in his hand,
Ready to fight in the battle.
You would never believe the sights that he saw,
As he heard the gunshots rattle.

He ran through the field, ready to fire,
His leg was wounded like hell.
Blood pouring, dripping to the ground,
The corpses disgusting with such a vile smell.

It was one dark night, when the moon was low
And a storm was brewing in the sky.
The trees were wildly blowing in the air,
The leaves were being hurled up high.

The poor man knew his time had come,
A bullet hit him in the chest.
As he died, he said his goodbyes
And then was put to rest.

David Carter (13)
Langley Park School For Boys

THE WORLD AT THE BOTTOM OF THE SEA!

In the deep, dark depths
Of the big, blue sea,
There is a great big world,
That's coming alive for me.

Life lies hidden in the rocks
And in the reefs of coral too,
Light flickers like a moving picture,
The weight of water is like glue.

It's a paradise of colours and shade,
Seaweed and plants abound, unplanned,
Eyes shine and flicker between the rocks
And bodies shimmer through the sand.

Fantastic creatures swim all day,
Beneath the power of the wave,
I think they love their watery world,
Which only strong men can brave.

Life exists in these deep, dark depths,
Where nearly only nature rules,
It's just as well they can't see above,
A land dominated by fools.

Alexander McNeill (12)
Langley Park School For Boys

CHALLENGING TIMES

Confused and helpless, but what could I do?
Shotguns rattled, not caring for the cost,
The noise was horrific as people were shot,
No one took charge and be responsible for lives lost.

Surrounded from all sides, we had now lost,
That glimmer of hope that we would survive,
Was now nothing but an empty feeling inside,
For months we had fought, always with a patriotic drive.

We marched for days without rest-bite and food,
The injured never made the day after,
The ones who were tired and lagged behind were shot,
We could see the German scum, were smiling and taunting us.

We marched in through the camp, staring ahead,
Armed soldiers were everywhere, looking ahead,
Thrown into the non-lit hovels, without any beds,
We sat there waiting for the sun to rise, with heavy heads.

We were called out early, standing in lines,
Being interrogated one by one,
Pressing for information that they couldn't find,
We were toy soldiers, who never rebelled, following signs.

The family at home, how would they cope?
Not knowing whether I was dead or alive,
The three little kids, they wouldn't know who was dad,
May would be strong and muddle on through, just like my comrades.

The group called the SAS were coming,
We just didn't know what we should expect,
Imagining the torture that we might go through,
The thoughts that rushed through my head were unimaginable.

Four years I had been stuck in this hellhole,
Living to survive, that day that I woke,
That time had come though; I was going to be free,
All of those bad memories, I am putting behind me.

Thomas McClinton (14)
Langley Park School For Boys

GROTESQUE GRUDGES

All evil grudges fester frantically fast
And before long they're there to last.
They cunningly plan what they want you to do,
While mysteriously turning others' backs upon you.

Grudges constantly gnaw at the back of your mind,
Seeing what new hellish delights they may just find.
They change what you would normally see and hear
And turn it into something that makes you not care.

They spawn from prejudice, jealousy and hate,
Before quickly spreading and getting rid of your mates.
They build up frustration then suddenly let it all go,
Showing no remorse or regret for any caused woe.

A friend soon becomes your most despised foe,
And an enemy somehow seems even worse.
All because of a split second judgement or action,
Done by you and your now demented, malevolent head.

Please take my humble yet harshly learned advice,
And suppress putrid opinions created out of mistrust.
When you look back I think you'll be most pleased,
As after all you helped stop a spiteful disease.

Adam Peters (14)
Langley Park School For Boys

A BALLAD OF THE TITANIC

People thought it was cool
She was built to be unsinkable,
But then came the unthinkable,
But then came the unthinkable

She was sailing along fine
She was owned by the White Star Line
She would arrive in no time
She would arrive in no time

The weather was really cold
'Iceberg ahead' the sailors were told
The iceberg hit the ship's soul
The iceberg hit the ship's soul

Water poured through the holes
Water splashed the engine room's coals
She would not now reach her goal
She would not now reach her goal

People thought it was cool
She was built to be unsinkable,
But then came the unthinkable,
But then came the unthinkable

Carpathia was called
Carpathia's engine roared
So many people mourned
So many people mourned

But the rescue ship was too late
It had been the great Titanic's fate
Die did most of her freight
Die did most of her freight

People thought it was cool
She was built to be unsinkable,
But then came the unthinkable,
But then came the unthinkable.

Edward Feist (13)
Langley Park School For Boys

THE RAGING SEA

The ship was flat, no wobble at all,
Sailed by the captain who stood so tall.
In the channel, halfway to France,
Was when the ship began to dance.

Up and down, left to right,
The weather was beginning to give us a fright.
The wind began to snatch at the sails,
This is another of those numerous gales.

The ship struggled onto its brink,
Suddenly the ship began to sink.
The water rushed in through the holes,
We all stood frozen like big toy dolls.

Was this the end? I could not tell.
This was as bad as fiery hell.
The ship sucked us down, to our grave.
We were all dead, too late, too late to save.

The sea was flat, no wave very tall,
Pleased it had managed to kill us all.

Tim Kay (12)
Langley Park School For Boys

FISH - NON-EXISTENT

He looked forward to the day ahead,
He was now all in good stead.
The fish was out there, east maybe west,
He had to beat all the rest.

Now the bait was all set up and packed,
Maybe the fish will be sacked.
So, start the engine and off he goes,
Will he come back; we don't know.

So out he goes into the blue sea,
Out he goes where he is free.
Miles and miles out he does go,
Out of your eyesight; *oh no!*

Now he is out there all on his own,
And the sea turned a weird tone.
There's no one about to scream and shout,
Please may a fish now just sprout.

The fish weren't out there, they don't exist,
They aren't added to the list.
Is it due to the climate changes?
Young fish, old fish, new ranges.

Off he moved to different places,
Up and down to new spaces.
Lots of money on petrol was spent,
Deep and shallow he now went.

But still no fish did come now to thee,
But he did stay just to see.
Ho haddock, no cod, nothing is there,
Who's given the fish a scare?

No fish were out there from any sets,
Back he comes with empty nets.
So, back he came to the lonely shore,
But to come back he's not sure.

When he is back the business is dead,
So now he is not ahead.
He comes back with a tear in his eye
And he now just wonders, why?

Anthony Plummer (14)
Langley Park School For Boys

A SCAR FOR LIFE

War: the pain of the world,
The endless suffering,
The cries of the innocent,
The sins of the guilty.

The men march blind sighted,
The inflicted pain not cared of,
The dead men not heard of,
The machines have no feelings.

The lost limbs of the men,
The lost men of the wives,
The shed tears of the children,
The many wasted lives.

The endless catastrophes,
The endless misfortune,
The dead silent,
A futile war.

Matthew Vadis (14)
Langley Park School For Boys

THE BALLAD OF PEARL HARBOUR

Another day dawns on the coast of Hawaii,
Not a single person knowing what it will bring.
The birds in the sky are gracefully flying
And the fish in the water joyfully swim.

The innocent people rise to the light,
With a sudden spring in their hurried pace,
But little do they know that without a fight
Their lives will be ruined by an act of disgrace.

But the cowards emerge before it gets late,
Their planes storming in through the thick white clouds.
Just a few minutes before it turns eight,
The Japanese attack with a mighty sound!

One bomb dropped and then another,
Destroying Pearl Harbour as it sleeps.
The mighty ships stand tall like brothers
And slowly crumble as they begin to weep.

Rumbling noises echo through the skies,
Tearing the American fleet apart.
The Japanese are cheats but tremendously wise,
Stabbing US military straight through the heart.

Chaos! Chaos! Everywhere,
One bomb here, one bomb there.
Screaming children running through the street,
Torn up lovers dying to meet.

But slowly the planes drift away
And the President says he will make them pay
And for leaving Pearl Harbour in this way,
America declared war the very next day . . .

David Hayes (13)
Langley Park School For Boys

THE WYRM'S LAIR

Desolation surrounds it
Scorched is the ground
Skulls litter the Earth
Placed by the king who wasn't crowned
Death hangs in the air
The stench of rotting flesh
Pungent, wretched, vile smell
Oozes out of every crevice
Deeper we delve into the recesses
Locked in the bowels of the mountain
Trapped in a black hole
Pulled by primal forces within
Now wading knee deep
In the carcasses of the defunct
Traitors, blasphemers, heretics
All in the gaping jaws of Hell were ducked
Still drawn by unearthly forces
You plunge unwillingly towards the inevitable
Demonic imps of ill thought
Plaguing the mind of the feeble
Legendary in ancient fable
Scourge of all things pure
Devouring the souls of the weak
Drawn in like moths by the treasure's lure
The Wyrm, the root of all malevolence
Curiosity becomes your bane
Underworld's fire now roasting your soul
Prematurely stole from the land of the sane
Now slain is he as all that dare
Trespass in the Wyrm's Lair.

Cyprian Rangel (14)
Langley Park School For Boys

THE BALLAD OF SEPTEMBER 11TH 2001

In New York, 9 o'clock, September 11th,
There was an awful act of crime,
There happened an attack, which could never be forgiven,
The Twin Towers of Manhattan fell down.

2 hijacked planes filled with people in hundreds,
Hit the north and south towers with force,
Within these planes men with knives killed, acting like dunderheads,
The victims made one last call to home.

I remember seeing on television
These pictures of destruction and horror,
I wondered how a human could make that decision,
But now it's all too late.

After they'd been hit, smoke billowed out,
People were jumping out windows,
Then they imploded with dust flying about,
It will take days for it to clear.

When we thought it was all over, it wasn't,
2 more planes then came down,
Has it all finished? I bet it hasn't,
Now we see what's next.

Who would have done this crime?
Are there people in the world today
Who think that it is as fine as sitting down to dine?
What sad idiots!

As the wreckage is cleared now,
We start to point our fingers,
Will these people strike again
Or just go into hiding?

It seems they may be more
And now we're in control,
It looks like there may be a world war,
Damn those fanatics!

David Jani (14)
Langley Park School For Boys

MY BOX

I will put in my box;

The glow of a glittering pearl at the bottom of the ocean,
The joy of a mother seeing her first newborn baby,
The sound of a seashell put close to my ear
And the power of love inside your heart.

I will put in my box;

The warmth of the boiling sun,
The feeling of gentle summer rain
And the beauty of a country view.

I will put in my box;

The excitement of coming into the world,
The innocence of a tiny girl
And the triumph of a battle won.

My box will be fashioned of;

The skin of the whitest white tiger
And the ice at the back of a comet.

I will hide my box;

In a miniscule cottage,
In the corner of a contented boy's eye.

Robert Outram (13)
Langley Park School For Boys

BALLAD: DEATH OF THE TWINS

It was a bright and cheerful day;
Cars moved around at well slow paces.
People came to work inside me;
With cheery smiles upon their faces.

My twin brother is also awake;
Our financial fires igniting.
I feel awake, life feels good;
The day feels really exciting.

On the horizon, I see a plane;
Moving so fast, like in a race.
Then it turns around and speeds towards me
And hits me hard, square in the face.

Arghh! It hurts! My face bleeds smoke
And all the workers inside me squeal.
Fires crack and burn inside me;
Of my insides, they make a meal.

Soon enough, another plane comes
And hits my brother in the chest.
He bleeds smoke and fires rage
Inside of him and all the rest.

The workers are all in a panic;
Some die of burns, some of fright.
Some just can't take it anymore
And just jump out from a great height.

Then my brother draws his last breath
And crashes down to the floor.
Of all the hundreds already killed;
Dead are thousands more.

My suspension now begins to creak;
To a building's death, I am bound,
Thousands of people still inside
Crash down with me to the ground.

It *was* a bright and cheerful day;
Cars now stopped, none took flight.
People looked on, with horrified looks;
Gone were the buildings of financial might.

Stephen Banfield (13)
Langley Park School For Boys

SHADOW

The shadows creep and crawl amongst us,
They stalk our every step and move
And when the sun is low in the orange sky they come out to play,
Releasing the harboured evils banished by the golden sun,
The shapeless, lifeless figures fester in hollow faces,
In the corner of every room,
Outside every bedroom window,
And in the twisted, shattered, fragmented caverns of everybody's
Mind and soul,
They incapacitate us with fear and hate,
They taunt us,
Pushing us over the edge into a land where the sane dare not tread
Or even look upon,
Their long, skinny fingers crawl over our pale flesh
And run through our hair,
Lifting each one gently from the scalp,
But all is forgotten when the gentle newness of day comes and wipes
The salty tears from our faces,
We are safe,
But not for long.

Jack Martin (14)
Langley Park School For Boys

THE BALLAD OF ANNE BOLEYN

In 1507, Anne was sent on an important day,
Born was a woman who kept King Henry at bay.
Her family for it could not reign,
But they would never be so lucky again.

In 1519 she was sent to France,
She seemed never to exit that trance.
An intelligent, elegant woman was made,
To think, she ended life under the blade!

On her return, courted by the king,
Twenty-four seven he would constantly ring.
His marriage with Catherine was falling apart,
He needed a new queen jewel in his heart.

Anne Boleyn, beautiful she could be,
Had a good life and well-off was she.
Well-spoken and clever, Henry did find,
But in the end her life was just blind.

Accepting his vow for marriage,
All she needed was no other miscarriage.
Secretly married with an amazing ring,
Eventually Catherine divorced the king.

But her honour was being declined,
As forceful King Henry wined.
A baby boy thee must bring,
But Henry was having another fling.

Another disappointment Anne brought,
Which upon led Henry to another bad thought.
High treason, high treason you bring unto me,
This thought just covered King Henry in glee.

On May 15th, Anne was tried,
She thought it was time she'd just have to bide.
Then in her defence, found was a crack,
And another life ended with an almighty *whack!*

Keir Ferguson (13)
Langley Park School For Boys

MY KIND OF MUSIC

People say I'm crazy and it's a load of rubbish!
I say it's my kind of music.

Mum says, 'Turn it down.'
But Dad says, 'Turn it up.'
I can't hear them it's so *loud!*

It's fast, furious, wacky and weird,
Some people can't stand it,
Now that's my kind of music.

Turning it on, waiting for it to explode,
Like a dynamite stick,
Now that's my kind of music.

It's my music . . . rock music.

Nicholas Brabner (13)
Langley Park School For Boys

THE BALLAD OF CASSIE BERNALL

It was a normal Colorado day,
One of the states in the USA
And Cassie Bernall left for school,
But up above was an angel's dual.

The killer went and got his gun,
Because many believed in God's one son.
One thing in mind that was to kill;
He took his gun and looked so chilled.

Cassie went into her school library,
Just to do a bit of study.
Little did she know that shortly later,
Cassie Bernall would be a martyr.

The killer walked around the place,
Looking for Cassie's young, dear face.
He shot relentlessly, without a flinch,
The souls that the Devil did clinch.

The killer had already shot his gun,
Because many believed in God's one son;
One thing in mind that was to kill,
As he shot his gun he looked so chilled.

The killer walked up toward Cassie Bernall,
And said to her, 'I'll see you in Hell;
But one last thing, do you believe in God?'
When Cassie said 'Yes' he asked 'Why?' then shot!

Her lifeless body fell to the floor,
As her spirit went through Heaven's great door.
As she saw God's face, she realised then,
That life on Earth was so full of sin.

Back on Earth the police did come,
And got the killer and his gun.
Earlier that day nobody knew that later,
Cassie Bernall would leave school a martyr.

Daniel Leeves (13)
Langley Park School For Boys

LOVE IS . . .

A speedy snail,
Light iron,
A worm that can't dig,
A slow Ferrari,
A text book with no information,
A dark light,
A good criminal,
A gentle lion,
An Olympics with no events,
A hard sponge,
A soft bullet,
A transparent curtain,
A book with no words,
A football match with no ball,
A pen with no ink.

Matthew Clayton (12)
Langley Park School For Boys

THE SUN

Magnificent yellow and deep hot red,
From North to South, the sun is many a mile,
From its great power, we humans are bred,
But also that power can be hostile.
Its strength is great; it holds in line the Earth,
You can smell the strength of the sun in every breath,
It's been a very long time since its birth,
But longer still awaits before its death.
Against others - though - 'a dwarf' is named the sun,
The sun is tough, but not tough enough,
For danger awaiting is challenged by next to none,
Where the sun would fail, a super giant would laugh.
Like all things the sun must pay its toll,
For its home is the home of the largest black hole!

Rowan Lonsdale (13)
Langley Park School For Boys

LOVE POEM

Love is
A mystery, a puzzle that cannot be solved
And I will solve that puzzle
Just for you
As my heart is burning ice
The ice will go,
But the flame will stay
That flame is you.

Alex Batten (12)
Langley Park School For Boys

THE DAY OF DEATH

As the hundreds of boats sailed to the shores
Many men stared in terror, clutching guns
And the huge, great ship, slowly opens its doors
In one moment, death comes to fathers and sons
Men sprint in panic, bullets come down like rain
Screams of agony, screams of pain, sounds of war
Wasted innocent lives, as men die in vain
Soldiers clamber up the cliffs, as bombs soar
And then a sudden silence echoes the beach
The great defence defeated, many dead
Victory has come, the fort has been breached
A landscape of hell, the sands stained with red
    Men dying for freedom, country and king
    In Heaven, even the angels can't sing . . .

Sam Hudson (13)
Langley Park School For Boys

LOVE IS . . .

A slow race I'm trying to win for you.
When I look at you it's like a dark sun.
I've cut myself on a blunt knife for you.
When I run I'm like a fast tortoise.
When I step outside I'm stepping on hot snow.
Sick health comes when I'm not with you.
Heavy air keeps us apart.

Sam Sunderland (12)
Langley Park School For Boys

AMERICAN INCIDENT

Thousands died when towers went down,
On people's faces were more than a frown.
Millions cried
For the people that died
When the Towers went down.
Next the terrorists
Hit the Pentagon.
Hundreds died all in one,
Millions cried
For the people that died
On that fateful day.
People lie dead under the rubble,
All we want to know is
Who caused all this trouble?

Daniel Watson (11)
Langley Park School For Boys

LOVE

When in love lead is light
When I see the night seems bright
Gold is cheap to show I care for you
My love for you would scare a lion
When with you rain is dry because of your love
Deadly life separates us.

Daniel Malynn (12)
Langley Park School For Boys

TRAGEDY

New York vibrates as people turn round only to see a fireball,
There's nowhere to run, the devastation is done, or is it?
As another fireball sweeps the town, Pentagon and Twin
                                       Towers are down.
The police and ambulance men gather around while firefighters
                                       are already there.
The scene settled as the clouds darken and a blurry mist forms,
You see shadows come out just like ghosts, closer they come till you
                                 find out they are rescuers.
Thousands of loved ones perish away under New York rubble,
The ghosts and tales will haunt them now,
All because of this terror and a unforgiving man,
Still firefighters find hundreds and thousand of bodies,
Dead, alive and parted.

Christopher Lesflores (11)
Langley Park School For Boys

LOVE IS BEAUTIFUL

When I see you I can't hear the loud radio,
When I see you it's like watching ice burn.
I run like a fast slug to win a race for you.
Your eyes are like beautiful mud.
When I go into water with you it is so dry.
When I see you it's light in pitch-black.

Joseph Sutcliffe (12)
Langley Park School For Boys

THE BALLAD OF HE

His tiny eyes observe the world,
Everything seems a mystery,
This tiny blessing loved by all,
Becoming a part of history.

What prospects lie in store for him
And what will he do?
A life fulfilled with immense success,
Filled with happiness too.

Offspring lets off a great wail,
His distress alerts its mother.
'Whatever is the matter my lad?
You're crying is like no other.'

The infant's weeping comes to a halt:
Lying still in his bed,
Not a movement more does the baby make,
'Rest,' his mother said.

An hour later his mother comes up,
To check on her dear sweet lad,
Sees he's not moved a single inch,
Sense this could be bad.

She reaches up to check his pulse,
But cannot feel a beat,
This blessing that was once so great,
The heavens he's gone to meet.

James Wilson (13)
Langley Park School For Boys

IT HAPPENED LIKE THIS

It happened like this on a sunny afternoon,
This terrible tragedy occurred from out of the blue,
The Twin Towers, 110 stories high,
Stood gleaming, just waiting to die,
Thousands of people all strolled to work,
All suffered the day when that Afghan twerp
Decided to bring these great towers down.

In Boston airport, two flights to LA
Were hijacked without delay,
Two mad men I tell you, with turbans on their heads,
Flew straight to New York.

Air traffic control did nothing,
Their minds just a diddle,
But back on the plane,
The people were screaming,
Until everything was silenced when the great fireball struck,
Off the side of a once gleaming tower.

People who jumped from 50 stories high,
Suffered death, as those other people did,
It happened a little later,
It shrunk to the ground,
Firemen hustling and bustling around,
All is lost as the little tear drops,
The ash arises up to the sky,
I hope we remember why these,
Poor people died.

James King (11)
Langley Park School For Boys

THE SLAVE TRADE

Once long ago when I was nine,
I said to myself, 'I wanna be a man.'
I looked after pigs pretty fine
And all of this happened before my nightmare.

Then five years later I went into training,
I kept losing a wrestling match with a man,
But at least I was good at hunting
And all of this happened before my nightmare.

This nightmare is called the Slave Trade,
They take you from your home at night,
All this happens during a raid,
The nightmare known as the Slave Trade.

At the end of my training I had one more task,
I had to catch the crafty monkey,
I completed this and got the man-mask
And all of this happened before my nightmare.

I went back home to be a man
And possibly find a mate for me.
But I saw white man and I ran
And this was the start of my nightmare.

This nightmare is called the Slave Trade,
They take you from your home at night,
All this happens during a raid,
The nightmare known as the Slave Trade.

They chased me well into the forest,
They were slow but they had dogs,
Throughout the chase I did not have rest
And this was part of my nightmare.

They stuffed us on a ship, side by side,
Everyone around me was sick,
Then I slipped into a sleep and died
And that was the end of my nightmare.

This nightmare is called the Slave Trade,
They take you from your home at night,
All this happens during a raid,
The nightmare known as the Slave Trade.

Matthew Howard (13)
Langley Park School For Boys

TOWER OF TERROR

The Twin Towers on the ground,
A crashing noise, a mighty sound.

The day had just started
And the planes had departed.

George W Bush saying 'Calm down,'
To this devastated town.

The rubble and rocks fall to the ground,
In some people's eyes without a sound.

When people are crying,
Others are dying.

This has truly devastated me,
Could this be the start of World War III?

Michael Quigley (12)
Langley Park School For Boys

THE LITTLE ONE

Below hills of grass, soil and clay,
Strange little people lie.
Search for them high, low or far,
You won't find them if you try.

The little folk from underground,
Inquisitive though they may be,
Are stout of heart and wise in brain,
Yet still hard to see.

This story tells of a little one,
The world he wanted to see,
Adventurous were the folk of his town,
Not an exception was he.

He trekked across meadows, hills and dale,
His steed was very fair,
Not once id it try to jolt him off,
Taking him here and there.

Into a wood they galloped along,
Over many a stile.
Strange hustling noises they could hear,
So they hastened, mile by mile.

Deep in the heart of the startling wood,
His faithful horse stumbled.
A creak came from the bridge they were on,
It had started to crumble.

The young, demure little one,
Tumbled and suddenly fell.
Into a blood-stained foul-smelling place,
It looked like a living hell.

A squamous creature, slimy and grey,
Sauntered into the room.
Words failed the little one's tiny mouth,
This was to be his tomb.

He stood and gaped at the hideous thing,
Standing face to jaw.
He decided to put up a fight before death
And scoured the cold stone floor.

He stood upon a mangled bone,
Sharp was its end.
For a sword it would have to do,
Against this creature to fend.

The little one from a peaceful town,
Still knew how to fight.
Bold was he and strong his arm,
So he struck with all his might.

It seared through flesh, bone and marrow,
Came out the other side.
Though extremely strong this thrust was,
The thing had not died.

The little one, jubilant was he,
He turned to the room's back.
The thing reared up high to full extent,
Ready to attack.

The little one jumped way too slow,
It was just too late.
He got speared from back to front
And death was his fate.

Timothy Burton (13)
Langley Park School For Boys

MY BALLAD OF THE FA CUP

The biggest event of the year,
Everyone's excited,
For who will make it to the top,
It won't be United!
Last year the winner was Chelsea,
This year who will it be?
It's not gonna be United,
Just have to wait and see.
Silky skills - Thierry Henry,
Pace of Michael Owen,
It's really hard to make your mind
On where the Cup's goin'!
The millions of people roar,
The two coaches arrive,
Millions of pounds of talent,
FA Cup Final - live!
The whistle blows - the game is on,
There's tension everywhere,
Sound of the ball, roar of the crowd;
Switch off? You wouldn't dare!
Handball! Surely a penalty!
The referee says no!
The Arsenal players are fuming!
'Twas handball by Henchoz.
Chance after chance for the Arsenal,
But they cannot convert,
Denied a blatant penalty,
The Arsenal fans are hurt.
The ball's gone in! They've gone ahead!
The Arsenal hopes arise,
Freddie Ljungberg puts it away,
And that is no surprise!

Still the chances come for Arsenal,
But will it be enough?
Despite our 1-0 lead,
Last minutes will be tough.
Oh no! Disaster has just struck,
Michael Owen has scored,
We need a bit of magic from
The one Sylvain Wiltord.
Can you believe he's done it again!
It's in the back of the net,
With only three minutes to go,
But it's not over yet.
Those two goals from Michael Owen,
May cost the Arsenal dear,
The FA Cup looks out of reach,
The end is drawing near.
It's all over! The ref has blown,
The game was very tight,
The scousers ran away with it,
It really is not right.
Sick'ning sight of the FA Cup
Being lifted in the air,
No silverware this season for
The Arsenal - it's not fair!

Steven Eadon (13)
Langley Park School For Boys

TWIN TROUBLE

I came home from school one lazy night,
I walked through the door to get a big fright.
My mum was in tears my dad was amazed,
I couldn't work it out, now I was in a daze.
I walked into t he kitchen to hear the news,
Straight away I knew we were going to lose.
I stayed there watching for half an hour or so,
Until the next plane came in very low.
It struck the side of the second Twin Tower,
Then I knew the terrorists had power.
The first one dropped 20 minutes later,
The second one in unison twenty minutes after.
I hoped they would be alright,
But deep down I knew I wanted to fight.

Robbie Mathieson (11)
Langley Park School For Boys

CHRISTMAS DAY

When I wake up in the morning, I get my stocking and bring it down.
I wait for Mum, Dad and my sister to come down, then Dad gets the video or the camera on.
Then I open my presents.
My sister opens her presents.
My sister gives presents to me, Mum and Dad.
Then I give presents to Mum, Dad and my sister.
Then Mum and Dad open their presents.
Then I play with my new toys, for the whole day.
Put them away at the end of the day.
Have a dream on the same night.
Merry Christmas everyone!

Vimal Patel (11)
Marjorie McClure School

HALLOWE'EN

Bring a candle!
  Bring a light -
It must be Hallowe'en
  Tonight

I saw a pixie
  Small and fine
Dancing
  On the washing line . . .

I saw a witch
  Go riding high
On her broomstick
  Through the sky . . .

I saw a giant
  Ten feet wide
With half a dozen
  Ships inside . . .

I saw a fairy
  Like a dream
Top the milk
  And sip the cream . . .

I saw a goblin
  Plump and brown
Turn the church clock
  Upside down

Come as quickly
  As you can –
I saw the back
  Of a bogey man!

Caraline Thompson (13)
Marjorie McClure School

I Washed My Face In Engine Oil

I washed my face in engine oil
By last Thursday it had sprouted a big red boil

I plucked my eyebrows with toothpicks
When I woke my cat's whiskers had flicks

I took a bath in lemon juice
And ate some strawberry mousse

I washed my hair with suntan lotion
And started up a cancan motion

I cut my nails with chopsticks
And filed them with a Twix

I polished my shoes with plant feed
And my cherry plant started to seed

I washed my feet with pepper and salt
I turned around and my dog had started to moult

I brushed my teeth with ketchup and a shaver
I was put in a psychiatric unit for mental behaviour

I combed my hair with a chrysanthemum
And started up the National Anthem.

Francesca Duff (11)
Marjorie McClure School

Under The Ocean

Way, way down under the ocean
The fish all swim in one big motion
Beneath the surface of the water
Lived a seahorse and her daughter

The starfish creeps along the seabed
All bright and orange looking to be fed
Every minute of every day
New colours appear in many a way.

Hannah Louise Payne (11)
St Anselm's Catholic School, Canterbury

SUNSHINE

My dreams and my heart
are full of fragments of disintegrated
memories,
good and bad,
filled with love and hope in which my parents bring,
through protection and love.
My parents bring sunshine, smiles and things,
a sunflower like a beam of light,
makes a sense of warmth spread
over my shady heart.

Then like a needle piercing through flesh,
I argue, with what was once a beautiful treasure.
My parents . . . in a bad mood!
Creates havoc when they find me
knee-high in spiralling phone bills!
I wish then,
that I was that small golden sunflower,
that does not give me the chills,
but gives me love, protection and forgiveness,
whenever I am down.

Sophia Moffatt-White (13)
St Anselm's Catholic School, Canterbury

MUM AND ME

I love my mum
  as much as the sun.

S he loves me
  even when she's angry with me.

O verall she's the best
  much better than lemon zest.

B ethany is my name
  my mum was overjoyed when I came.

E mbarrassment comes part of the pack,
  but that's what I lack.

L ove is happiness that's what it's about
  love is nicer than eating trout.

Bethany Clegg (12)
St Anselm's Catholic School, Canterbury

LIFE

When you are a baby your parents hold you tight
Feed you when you're hungry, cuddle you through the night
Your first day at school with shiny new shoes
Mum and Dad at home time waiting for the news.

Growing up is difficult, sometimes with arguments and tears,
But parents always by your side everlasting through the years.

Respect your mum and dad
Talk with love and care
For when the day is over they will always be there.

Dominic Alexander (12)
St Anselm's Catholic School, Canterbury

THE BLUE WHALE

Sharks go *snap!*
Jellyfish go sting!
All these animals are beneath the dark sea.

Dolphins chat, chat!
Fish bubble, bubble!
All these things can cause trouble!

Sea lions make noise!
Penguins just waddle!
All these animals sometimes paddle!

But under the sea,
There is an animal . . .
Who doesn't even make a sound.

Who could it be?

Where shall we look?

It's the . . .

Blue whale.

Charlotte Stiffell (11)
St Anselm's Catholic School, Canterbury

NEVER SAW, NEVER SEEN

Never saw, never seen
Work took over where play should have been
A child so lonely, no parents to please
Joyful times of sincerity and glee
Were long passed
Replaced by work where play should have been.

Jack Martyn (12)
St Anselm's Catholic School, Canterbury

PARENT AND CHILD

A child needs love,
A parent needs a heart.
A child needs a glove,
When the weather gets cold.

You need love,
You need a heart,
Happiness, fun, joy,
We bring it all.

A child needs a smile,
Once in a while,
A parent needs one,
So you can see it from a mile.

You need love,
You need a heart,
Happiness, fun, joy,
We bring it all.

A child needs caring,
A parent needs respecting,
You need the comfort,
Which is a kiss and a hug.

You need love,
You need a heart,
Happiness, fun, joy,
We bring it all.

A perfect parent,
A perfect child,
Mix it all together,
And you get a smile.

You need love,
You need a heart,
Happiness, fun, joy,
We bring it all.

Giselle Hyam (13)
St Anselm's Catholic School, Canterbury

BOY TO A MAN

They scream and shout
And always pout
They cry all night
Want to start a fight.

As the days go on
The years pass by
The child grows up
To a man with a beard.

As they grow up the stress level rises
The asking for money
Happens more often.

You never would have thought
That things were that hard,
But look what I've brought up
A baby to a man.

I look back at the years
All the tears that I shed
And still to come the things that I dread,
But all of it was worth it
As a person I am proud.

Natalie Shilling (13)
St Anselm's Catholic School, Canterbury

BEDTIME

A little girl all dressed ready for bed,
In comes the parent to kiss her goodnight.
A little story and the bedbugs won't bite,
At the end of the story, she turns off the light.

The child's all scared, tucking in when it's dark,
She's thinking of nice things,
Like animals, flowers and that.

A little girl all dressed ready for bed,
In comes the parent to kiss her goodnight.
A little story and the bedbugs won't bite,
At the end of the story, she turns off the light.

In the morning, I woke up quickly,
Light shining through the window.
My eyes full of sleet and light,
Out of my pyjamas, oh good it's so bright.

A little girl all dressed ready for bed,
In comes the parent to kiss her goodnight.
A little story and the bedbugs won't bite,
At the end of the story, she turned off the light.

Sitting down round the table,
With my mum in the kitchen,
My dad has the knives and forks
And I'm sitting, waiting.

Victoria King (12)
St Anselm's Catholic School, Canterbury

VERY DEEP DOWN UNDER THE SEA

Think about the whales
Those ginormous creatures
Who could destroy an army
Just by opening their mouths

Deep down under the sea
Where everything amazes me
The shells and creatures
The rocks and caves
The splashing water
And the roaring waves

Think of the sharks
And those sharp, jagged jaws
A mouth of a demon
With a thousand chainsaws

Think of the caves
And their dark, deep depths
You don't know what's down there
Even divers don't dare to go down there

Deep down under the sea
Where everything amazes me
The shells and creatures
The rocks and caves
The splashing water
And the roaring waves.

Josephine Kirwan (11)
St Anselm's Catholic School, Canterbury

MY PARENTS ARE ALIENS

My mum and dad are good to me,
A good child I must be.
They shout at me to do things right,
Otherwise I don't see the daylight.

When they are ill
I take care of them,
And they will do the same for me.

They embarrass me when they bring old things up,
Like when I was always saying
'Do as you are told.'

If I am sad they will make me laugh,
Tell me till I have had enough.

I shout at them when they annoy me,
But they always stop me getting
Stung by a bumblebee.

Sophie Wood (12)
St Anselm's Catholic School, Canterbury

UNDER THE SEA

Down in the sea the fish start to flee
The fearsome sharks are coming
Up upon the land penguins are jumping
The killer whale is hunting
Up upon the surface a boat is killing
Its nets trapping anything in its way,
But on the beach humans safe and having fun
For they are not the hunted.

Liam Bestic (11)
St Anselm's Catholic School, Canterbury

THE TUNA

Tuna swimming fast
Hunting in the sea which is last
Chasing, hunting the small fishes
Eating what he wishes.

He makes quick dashes for fish shapes,
In which he finds the hook's sharpness
Through his gill not in his will.

In what hole or surface wave
Or in what underwater cave
Jumping on the surface
Trying to get the hook from his face
The tuna was pulled afloat
Its life ended on the boat.

Ashley Dadd (12)
St Anselm's Catholic School, Canterbury

SEA THE EXPERIENCE

Visit to the seaside full of *fun!*
Hear the rhythm of the sea in the rough seashell
Swim underwater with the *scaly*, slimy fish
Fly in the salty wind like a chirping seagull
Bluey-green waves crashing on the rocks
Spiky yellow coral in the depths of the ocean
What would it be like at the bottom of the sea?
Or soaring out of the *water* like a grey blue
Whale?

Helen Underwood (12)
St Anselm's Catholic School, Canterbury

OCEAN

Crashing waves
Is like the rhythm of the sea
Breaking of ice
The ocean is where I would like to be.

Dolphins jumping in and out
Is like the rhythm of the sea
Other fish swimming about
The ocean is where I would like to be.

Whales under the ocean
Is like the rhythm of the sea
Watching fish swim in a motion
The ocean is where I would like to be.

Asti Speed (11)
St Anselm's Catholic School, Canterbury

THE DOLPHIN

The dolphin swims in the big deep blue,
Not alone but with others too!

When the dolphin swims it does it with ease,
Feeling the lovely gentle breeze.

The dolphin jumps in and out of the waves,
It could carry on for days and days.

The dolphin eeks all day long,
Singing its own dolphin song.

Finally it stops for a fishy takeaway,
Then it starts swimming for another day.

Jessica Driscoll (11)
St Anselm's Catholic School, Canterbury

THE BEAUTIFUL BEAST

God made whale in the night
When all the stars were bright
There was no life at sea
Not as far as man could see

The mighty hand pulled out some clay
Which had been played with for a year and a day
He poured the blood of a lonely seal
He thought to himself who would touch and feel
This beautiful mammal who is gentle and calm,
But yet can fit into my palm.

God made whale in the night
When all the stars were bright
There was no life at sea
Well, not as far as man could see.

Emma Benson (11)
St Anselm's Catholic School, Canterbury

DOWN IN THE OCEAN

Down in the ocean where all the fish sleep
They open their eyes and peep
Down in the ocean in the coral
Some sharks come down and cause a quarrel
Who can catch the biggest fish?
Who can eat the biggest dish?
Down in the ocean some dolphins swim
They like to swim and play and sing.

Rosie Burgess (11)
St Anselm's Catholic School, Canterbury

SOON

As the krill dart through water,
The whale is coming,
As the seagulls glide through the air,
The whale is coming,
As the dolphins cluster fish,
The whale is coming,
As the sharks scare crabs,
The whale is coming
As the eels mimic snakes,
The whale is coming
Suddenly
24 tonnes
Of power
Devour
Millions
Nothing's left
The whale has come!

Jonathan Murray (11)
St Anselm's Catholic School, Canterbury

WAVES

Windy, wet and cold
Icy on the breeze
Huge, colossal, immense
Waves full of life
Glittering fish
Colourful
Bright
Foamy, splashing, salty waves
Sing beautiful songs of the sea.

Sophie Cartwright (11)
St Anselm's Catholic School, Canterbury

THE SEA

We are of the ocean
This is what we call home
Is a water planet
From space it's a cerulean sphere
Of glittering liquid
Iced with water planet

Our hearts beat
In a rhythm set by the waves
That splash along the shore

The sea is our great mother
Who nurtures us and watches us
In her still, deep sea
To be in the ocean
And dive beneath the waves

Then return to the sea for the long voyage home.

Ryan Smith (11)
St Anselm's Catholic School, Canterbury

RHYTHM OF THE SEA

Curled, long, speedy, fish, fish
Rhythm in the sea, splash, splash
Scuttling shark, silky, scaly
All the fish come out
To see the morning glee
Salty seawater, rough, smooth
Long, smooth seaweed, stretched or scrunched
Shh, you can hear the waves, some big, others small.

Jonathan Hoyle (11)
St Anselm's Catholic School, Canterbury

DEEP BLUE SEA

When the waves are crashing,
And the lightning's flashing,
You're out in the deep blue sea,
When the dolphins are diving,
The sardines have a hard job surviving,
You're out in the deep blue sea.

They're all so amazing,
Colours are ablazing
And the feeling . . . magical.

When thousands of fish are passing
And the shark's appetite seems everlasting,
You're out in the deep blue sea,
When the seals are playing,
The hungry whales are waiting,
You're out in the deep blue sea.

They're all so magnificent,
Each one of them significant
And the feeling . . . wonderful.

Joe Vallely (11)
St Anselm's Catholic School, Canterbury

THE SEA

Seagulls circle round the land,
Waves crashing on the sand,
Sharks swimming in the sea,
Making other creatures flee,
Children enjoying the seaside sun,
Playing, laughing and having fun!

Mark Fellowes (11)
St Anselm's Catholic School, Canterbury

PENGUINS

Funny-looking, clumsy waddle
Hunched back, webbed feet splayed
Toddle to water's edge

Plunging clumsily, splishing, splashing
Into the cold, cold sea
Flying through the water
Gracefully moving

Fear! Fear! The killer whale is here

Twirling, whirling, round and round
Out of the water quick as they can

Fear! Fear! The killer whale is here.

Robert Coles (11)
St Anselm's Catholic School, Canterbury

THE WHALE'S SONG

The ocean was once full of whales
They were as big as hills
As peaceful as the moon
And as smooth as the sea
As large as mountains
Bluer than the sky
And they could sing
Loud and clear
Across the sea
Singing your name.

Rosanna Hosker-Thornhill (11)
St Anselm's Catholic School, Canterbury

FEARLESS

As the shark roams across the sea
Fearless
Quiet
Waiting for the right moment
Seeking for its prey
It finds the moment
The seal
A common dish for the shark
The shark approaches the seal
Pretending not to be interested
The chance comes
The shark takes it
It misses
It shows the shark isn't the greatest
Animal on the Earth.

Lauren Morgan (11)
St Anselm's Catholic School, Canterbury

THE SEA

Sharks fighting
Fish fleeing like lightning

Coral reef's beauty
Some fish loopy

Sardines, mackerel
Dogfish too

This frenzy of fish
Is hard to miss.

Michael Baker (11)
St Anselm's Catholic School, Canterbury

SEA CREATURES

Waves crash, crash, dolphins splash, splash, birds flap, flap
Fish clap, clap, under the water see the
Creatures, also see their lovely features.
Waves crash, crash, dolphins
Splash, splash, birds
Flap, flap,
fish clap,
clap.

Hannah Wilford (11)
St Anselm's Catholic School, Canterbury

FIRST DAY AT SCHOOL

F   irst friend was Dene
I   started on Wednesday
R   eally noisy children
S   chool staff all new
T   ired children

D   usty classroom
A   ll fatty smells
Y   oung children frightened

A   t school on time
T   ime is going slowly

S   orry about the lonely children
C   anteen was really noisy
H   ard work
O   ffer to open the doors
O   nly one hour to go
L   ast, it is home-time.

Simone Brazier (13)
The Cedars Pru School

I DON'T WANT TO GO TO SCHOOL TODAY

I don't want to go to school today
Cos I hate it,
Cos it's too far to walk,
Cos it's dinners,
Cos it's rugby,
Cos it's anything.

I might go to school today
Cos it's alright,
Cos it's DT,
Cos it's maths,
Cos it's reading,
Cos it's . . . OK.

I think I will go to school today
Cos there's pool,
Cos there's PE,
Cos there's English,
Cos I can use the library,
Cos the history lessons are good.

Tomos Lewis (13)
The Cedars Pru School

WEEPING

On the train, off to war, both his parents weeping,
On the campsite, training hard, still his parents weeping,
Gets his gun, on the boat, off to do his duty,
His parents keep on weeping,
On the field, running through, no sign of them yet,
Bang . . .
Everybody weeping.

Daniel Macken (12)
The Cedars Pru School

I Don't Want To Go To School Today

I don't want to go to school today
Cos I hate it,
Cos it's getting up,
Cos it's getting ready to go to school,
Cos it's work,
Cos it's anything.

I might go to school today
Cos it's alright,
Cos it's woodwork,
Cos it's maths,
Cos it's playing pool,
Cos it's . . . OK.

I think I will go to school today
Cos there's break,
Cos there's walking to school,
Cos there's badminton,
Cos I can play hockey,
Cos it's the last day of term.

Phillip Fagg (13)
The Cedars Pru School

Scary House Poem

Walked up to the house on a cold, dark night,
Something moved in the trees, made my heart pound with fright.
Went through the door and felt a chill,
Should I now start writing my will?
Went upstairs via a squeaky door,
Something scurried across the floor.
Entered a room with a four-poster bed
And a huge chest that rose above my head.
It was as though I had walked into a scary show
And now it was my time to go.

Rebecca Halls (12)
King Ethelbert School

THE HOUSE DOWN MY ROAD

The house down my road
Was very, very old,
The garden was creepy and dark
And inside there was an old water fountain
With a statue whose eyes seemed to follow you.
The front door was green
And not very clean with spiders and slugs all over it.
I could not get in through the door,
So I climbed up the ivy and went through a window.
When I got in, I couldn't believe it,
There were 12 clean black suits.
I went down the stairs completely confused,
Down the stairs I saw a telephone,
I tried it and pressed a few numbers
And guess what happened?
A door opened to reveal a lift,
I thought if I went down there it would be bad, so I ran.
So remember,
Not everything is what it seems to be.

Gregory Bayliss (12)
King Ethelbert School

56 CROXLEY STREET

How would you like to see a ghost?
I know a house that is its host.
Croxley Street is a haunted house,
So if you visit be as quiet as a mouse.

It creaks and groans as you move about,
Be careful not to scream or shout,
Be warned, don't wake the ghost within,
For surely that would cause a din.

Don't stay too long or you'll never get out
Of that horrible haunted house,
Remember now, don't wake the ghost,
Or he will end up being *your* host!

Kayleigh Maxted (12)
King Ethelbert School

HALLOWE'EN SCHOOL

I woke up on a normal school day,
Except it was Hallowe'en,
I went to school, but on the way
Everyone was mean.

In the school corridor,
The lights went out,
It was getting more and more
Scarier, so I started to shout.

My teacher came running,
'What's wrong dear?'
I saw her face, so scary, so cunning,
Things were getting queer.

I went into my class,
There were bats, vampires and even ghosts,
Eyeballs in a jar of glass,
The teacher was sitting eating worms on toast.

I screamed, I sat up,
I was still in bed,
Everything was there, even my old cup,
'What a queer dream!' I said.

Amy Stevens (12)
King Ethelbert School

THE EMPTY HOUSE OF HORROR!

The house stood empty for so many years,
Hanging, just hanging over the piers,
The lamps outside had burnt to the ground,
Nobody entered, not even my hound.
Something was wrong, not quite right,
Caused by the moaning, moaned at night

The house stood empty for so many years,
Hanging, just hanging over the piers,
The floorboards creaked
And the rotting doors shrieked.
Something was wrong, not quite right,
Caused by the padlocked loft, it gives you a fright.

The house stood empty for so many years,
Hanging, just hanging over the piers,
Nobody knows who goes there and why,
I suppose there is more to it than meets the eye.
Something was wrong, not quite right,
Caused by the mist that challenged your sight.

James Tomlinson (12)
King Ethelbert School

THE EMPTY HOUSE

The empty house was dark and scary,
Everything looked gloomy and dead.
All the plants were brown and droopy,
They were dying, very slowly.

Pictures of people covered the walls,
Their eyes followed you in every direction.
The floors were dusty
And the rugs were stained.

All the doors to the bedrooms were locked,
With no key to be found.
The furniture had stated to fade,
Because of a small ray of light through the boarded-up window.

Jessica Dempsey (12)
King Ethelbert School

THE HOUSE OF NO RETURN

There it is over there, the house of no return,
It's cold and scary,
Gloomy and dark
And they say there's ghosts in there.
The house is tall and thin,
The gates are creaky,
The path is cracked
And my heart is beating fast.

As I said, there's ghosts in there,
The scary type you know,
They only come out at night
At dawn they turn to dust.
I think I see one looking at me,
That see-through face,
Those evil, evil eyes,
Oh I wish I was at home.

The slates are off the roof
And the windows are broken and smashed,
Kids have been in there,
Small, tall, thin and fat
And all have never been seen again,
Better run before I . . . get . . . caught.

Samantha Taylor (12)
King Ethelbert School

56 CROXLEY STREET

There was once an empty house
At the end of Croxley Street,
It was number 56.
In the garden was very tall grass,
It was knee-high and was brown,
There was a creaky, black gate,
That was hanging off its hinge,
The path was cracked,
The path was uneven
With snail trails on top.
There was once an empty house
At the end of Croxley Street,
It was number 56.
The outside of the house
Was crumbly,
Had a few bricks missing,
Smashed window
And had wooden shutters.
There was once an empty house
At the end of Croxley Street,
It was number 56.

Jodie Gee (12)
King Ethelbert School

NEW YEAR'S GHOST

If you step inside the house,
Be as quiet as a mouse,
You don't want to see what's lurking there,
She or it has a cold, icy stare.

He or it has long blond hair,
And she or it is lurking there.
This thing sits in a gloomy room,
Staring at the cold, grey moon.

Once a year on New Year's Day,
This she or it will have a way
Of getting rid of the unexpected,
Of which he, she or it is.

Kelly Marshall (12)
King Ethelbert School

GHOSTBUSTERS

I thought I saw a ghost
Appearing through the wall
I picked up the yellow pages
To think of who to call

I rang the Ghostbusters
They said they'll be over in a tick
I heard a spooky noise
And the lights began to flick

I went downstairs to see
When I heard the noises again
The door burst open and
The grandfather clock struck ten

A man stood in the doorway
And said 'Make us a cuppa tea!'
So I went into the kitchen
And made tea for three

'Come on lads get out ya gear
Show 'um what ya got
I hope we get our money's worth
Let's ghostbust this lot
Ghostbusters.'

Jessica Pettman (12)
King Ethelbert School

56 CROXLEY STREET

56 Croxley Street is dirty and damp,
It looks so sinister under the old street lamp.

There's dirt and grime on the wall,
I wouldn't be surprised if no one lived there at all!

Glass is shattered all on the floor.
I bet it's never been tidied up before!

The grass is taller than a block of flats,
There's fungi growing on the old porch flats.

Mould and fungi on the ceiling,
Always receiving that scary feeling.

People watching, people spying,
People looking, people eyeing.

Always trembling with lots of fear.
This poem's too scary, I'm out of here!

Lucy Cook (12)
King Ethelbert School

56 CROXLEY STREET

56 Croxley Street
Is a crooked place,
Its bricks are crumbled,
Its ceilings are cracked
And it's really, really dirty.

A strange and weird man lives there,
People say he isn't nice,
A little old lady said he killed her sweet cat.

He mustn't be keen on housework,
Except for in one room,
Which is very, very tidy,
The others are full of cobwebs.

What a dirty, horrible place
Is 56 Croxley Street.

Hayley Constable (12)
King Ethelbert School

THE OLD HOUSE

The house was dark,
it chilled the heart,
it had belonged to an old fart,
who was hit by a dart,
while eating some vindaloo.

The house is now empty,
except for a shandy and a hairy bit on the floor.
Make no mistake it was a piece of cake
that was left there for forty years.

The house was a sight,
but used to be mighty and bright.
But now it is disused,
battered and bruised
and falling into disrepair.

One day it will have fallen,
crumbled and broken
and will have a multi-storey car park
built on top.

William Mitchell (13)
King Ethelbert School

FRIENDLY IMAGINATION

Sometimes when I'm all alone,
I talk to my friend, Ted,
We talk out in the corridor,
We even talk in bed.
He sleeps in my hammock,
He sleeps on the drawers,
He sleeps on the clock.
When I'm all alone, I talk to Ted
Even though,
I know he's in my head.
Sometimes we talk
With everyone around,
Because no one hears a sound!

Kelly Marshall (12)
King Ethelbert School

THE HOUSE

This old crumbling house,
No living inside,
Once there were children,
But now they've all died.

It sits all alone,
On the dark street,
This abandoned old home,
No patter of feet.

Some say there are ghosts,
But no one really knows,
No one dares to enter,
This abandoned old home.

Natalie Jones (12)
King Ethelbert School

ANYONE THERE?

The silence was almost deafening,
Grazing on a field of heads
No one muttered
No one moved
A sea of silence
Faces glaring, scaring
Deliberately
Cutting the fuse of this arrival
To one so short, that it was barely there
Like Mars
It was there, had a fuse, but no one cared
A scraping noise caught the air
Brave, oh so brave
A chair pushed back and someone stood
'Hello,' I said.

Julie-Anne Whitaker (13)
Westwood Technology College

DEE P BLUE SEA

Deep below the deep sea lies
a whale half asleep waiting and
watching for his prey.
He may have to wait
more than a day,
but when he gets a bite
he wakes up in a fright.
He smiles with a little glee,
knowing he can gobble up
the deep blue sea.

Louis Smith (13)
Westwood Technology College

SILLY TINY

Tiny is a budgie! Budgie,
Who has a pretty cage.

She likes to keep her house clean,
Which puts her mummy in her rage.

We think we'll buy her a hoover
And plug it in the wall,
So she can hoover her feathers as they fall.

She talks to her mirror,
Without knowing how.
The boyfriend inside that goes
Cock-a-doodle-do.

Ballet is her favourite,
With one leg in the air.
Topple! Topple! Topple,
She tumbles through the air.

Julie Cairncross
Westwood Technology College

FRIENDSHIP

Friendship reminds me of a plant
It blossoms over time
The stages of the growth remind me of the first words
The first flower opening reminds me of the first interesting conversation
The leaves fluttering in the wind reminds me of the first joke
                                        we laughed at
Then the first time the flower closes reminds me of the first time
                                        we said goodbye.

Amie Murphy (11)
Westwood Technology College

THE SEA CAT

The sea is a playful cat,
Small, round and baby blue,
She plays on the beach all the day,
On the ocean and then the bay,
Patting the rocks gently with its paws,
Then gnawing a stone with its jaws,
As it travels, it eats the fish,
Gently making it their daily dish.

The calm sea settles for the night,
Hiding itself from any fright,
The night rises and the sun goes down,
As the sea begins to slowly drown,
Once again the day is over,
And everything is quiet on the cliffs of Dover.

Faye McColgan (13)
Westwood Technology College

THE SWIFT ROBBER

The wind was soft, so was the rain
The water dripping down the drain,
A cool breeze crept through the house,
Trying to be as quiet as a mouse.
Through the lock without a key,
A very swift burglar you will never see.
Creeping through the rooms and halls,
The breeze dies, the burglar falls.
No one knew he was there at all.

Lauren Sparkes (13)
Westwood Technology College